Call for Leadership

Call for Leadership

Effective Practices of Leaders in the Search for New Wisdom

Marty Zimmerman and Brad Johnson

ROWMAN & LITTLEFIELD
Lanham • Boulder • New York • London

Published by Rowman & Littlefield
A wholly owned subsidary of The Rowman & Littlefield Publishing Group, Inc.
4501 Forbes Boulevard, Suite 200, Lanham, Maryland 20706
www.rowman.com

Unit A, Whitacre Mews, 26–34 Stannary Street, London SE11 4AB

British Library Cataloguing in Publication Information Available

Library of Congress Cataloging-in-Publication Data
Names: Zimmerman, Marty | Johnson, Brad
Title: *Call for Leadership: Effective Practices of Leaders in the Search for
New Wisdom* / Marty Zimmerman and Brad Johnson.
Description: Lanham: Rowman & Littlefield, 2018.
Includes bibliographical references.
Identifiers: LCCN 2018000576 (print) | LCCN 2018001661 (ebook) |
ISBN 9781475841053 (Electronic) | ISBN 9781475841039 (cloth : alk. paper) |
ISBN 9781475841046 (pbk : alk. paper)
Subjects: LCSH: Leadership.
Classification: LCC HD57.7 (ebook) | LCC HD57.7 .J6433 2018 (print) |
DDC 658.4/092—dc23
LC record available at https://lccn.loc.gov/2018000576

∞™ The paper used in this publication meets the minimum requirements of American
National Standard for Information Sciences—Permanence of Paper for Printed Library
Materials, ANSI/NISO Z39.48-1992.

Printed in the United States of America

Contents

Preface

A PERSONAL NEW YEAR'S REFLECTION

What would compel you to crack open a book whose title begins A Call of Nature? Does this first phrase grab you? If yes, you answered the dinner bell. A call of nature typically refers to what came in must go out. A call of leadership requires us to consider what goes into our thinking, our believing, and ultimately, what goes into our behaviors, which manifest either that attraction of others to our genuine calling as a leader, or behaviors that manifest something which people can smell out as a pretense of leadership. This call from within speaks to becoming our natural selves when leading others. The more pretense, the farther away we get from this endeavor called leadership. Becoming and behaving from our more authentic self becomes part of our life's journey.

As we experience at various times and through this life's journey, a part of me became stuck while attending college. I was raised to rely on myself, me against the world, and found myself in a team-centric college environment. To gain the most of my college years, I needed to foster a sense of reliability and sustained interactive relationships with my peers. Doing so, I often found myself making progress, only to occasionally self-sabotage my efforts and limit my vulnerability. This reduced me.

One in particular welcomed me into his circle of trust during those college years. Yet after a while, it became obvious this was a good relationship I did not know how to nurture. I identified myself more as a loner in a world of collegiality. A loner, relying on myself, perhaps to preclude becoming betrayed by others, this need to feel protected, led to betraying what could have been.

How about you? We each share memories of how we participated in a life event that we later realize exposed the influence of our own personal limitations. Later in life, I heard reference to this same author characterized as an ultimate team player among my business peers. What happened following those years at Annapolis?

Self-reflecting, I recently heard a priest's sermon on blessings following the week after Christmas. He referred to a biblical expression (quoting Jesus), "Blessed are the poor in spirit." Father talked about how the opposite extreme might sound. What, after all, if Jesus was recorded saying, "Blessed are those who win the lottery?" Few of us would feel blessed.

Recalling perceived past failures, disappointments in static tense, as if it was, then it is, and so it shall be—rears a captive sense of remorse. When Camp Remorse establishes a foothold, negative images become more pronounced, short-circuiting the positively charged present and future waiting for us to discover and seize.

Yet the role model leadership behaviors and stories of leaders in these following pages indicate that remorse can visit and inform, but not encamp and take center stage. Remorse can inform and inflame new learning and new capacity from an expanded awareness of personal life's lessons. We do not give power to remorse. It rather gives power to the poor in spirit, and it blesses instead of curses.

The stories and reflections of leader practice, of leader being, come not from people who experienced life free of personal learning, free of personal hardship, full of doing it right the first time. Try to follow these stories similar to how the wise men followed the star—uncertain of your destination, yet fully invested in the journey.

Turn yesterday's lemons into tomorrow's lemonade. Make yesterday's remorse today's vision and tomorrow's application of strength—strength of listening, of empathizing, of courage in the face of desperate voices wanting to be heard, seeking recognition of a being from within. Clarifying, cajoling, confirming.

A question soliciting opportunity for the face of courage to show itself may be situations in which the question gets asked, "What becomes more important right now, to do the right thing? Or to do things right?" Determining the distinction between which side of this question assumes front stage at any time can clarify the need for courageous action, courageous conversation, courageous patience, courageous (fill in the blank).

The practices of leaders to learn from remorse, from lessons learned, and to apply new wisdom through what they think and do reveal the learned behaviors still patiently waiting for you and for me to discover, embrace, and become. Regardless of titles, of roles we play, when in tandem with others, we continue practicing and playing on this practice field of life.

For some of us, this practice field may only be 17 yards long, for others of us, 29 yards, yet again, 80 yards for some, and if you consider this being lucky—for some of us, our practice field stretches 100 yards, both end zones, and then some.

Through time, there has been a play executed that has caused fans in the stands to arise in ovation and applause at every single yard of the playing field. At what yard line do you execute? And as Jesus and others might imply, not for the applause.

Rather, as an acknowledgment of the blessing received, allowing strength to be revealed, arising from a humble heart poor in spirit and ready to offer and receive. Ready to adopt new leadership behaviors. Ready to expand on lessons learned and intentionally create new habits inspired by purpose. We always prepare to adopt a new way of being with another individual, with another group, with any situation as it arises.

As that post-Christmas 2017 sermon reminds us regardless of background or faith, blessed are the vulnerable, blessed are the poor in spirit. This suggests our triumphs come at a price—a price of recognizing our own limitations, as well as our strengths, and learning through reflection to change our behavior and be more than what logic and life would dictate.

Allow ourselves to notice something greater than each of us when revealing the way. Takes courage as a reader. Are you ready? If ready to answer the dinner bell, read on, seeking that which reveals itself to you. May our God bless.

Marty Zimmerman

Chapter 1

Role Model Leadership Evidence— What Works for You?

"WHAT IF THIS DOESN'T WORK?"

The following pages are written for you the reader as a means of offering choices—alternatives—in choosing how to respond when recognizing the appearance of being stuck in the same specific scenario, repeatedly. Will you hear advice? Yes, whether directly, or indirectly, through stories and from people who also live the struggles of life. Do you experience struggles?

Pro football Hall of Famer and coach Mike Singletary genuinely shares some of his struggles, our struggles. This book describes ways of behaving that enable leaders to navigate the struggle. They epitomize a quote by Mother Teresa, "I am not called to be successful, I am called to be faithful."

This book reveals the commitment and wonder of journeying in pursuit of one's calling as a leader. A commitment of faith that trumps certainty and retains our childlike view of life with wonder at seeing the possibilities along the way.

Leadership is not about perfection, or being right. It is about being effective. In the moment of being effective, sometimes this may not "feel" right. Hence, the work of leadership and the art of practicing leadership as a leader or as a human being.

The intent is not to wax. Rather, to polish. To polish what may work or not work from the previous life experiences of others, which can inform future leadership decisions moving forward, provided this newly expanded view of possibilities for action. Not so that you do something different. So that you have the ability to choose to react or respond in a different way, *in the moment*.

This takes courage and ongoing awareness, beyond understanding what we share among the pages of this parchment to follow.

But what if, after reading and even trying some new practices, this just does not work?

Then as our current president might suggest, "You're fired." Not as a permanent ending. Rather as a means to moving forward!

What if you are called to be faithful instead of being successful? How would this shift your orientation toward leadership practice? What Mother Teresa states in essence defines your journey, your effort. Take heart. Look for a final quote from Mother Teresa on the last page of this book. Seek promise through these pages, and keep up the good fight, keep running the good race. And take some walks and side trips on occasion!

A thought for you the reader—Have you already acted in immediate gratification, and checked out the quote on the last page? Or have you decided to withhold seeking the definitive quote, while enabling your curiosity and anticipation to be enjoyed over the length of reading this book?

On the subject of immediate gratification, the author knew this wonderful man, a financial columnist, Don McNay, who referred to an experiment called the marshmallow story.

How many of us work on our self-control as a means of personal development? How could this manifest itself in the experience of our lives and our leadership? I share an excerpt of Don McNay's story here:

The New Yorker published a 2009 story about the psychology of delayed gratification.

It discussed a group of 4 year-old nursery school students who were part of a study done at Stanford University in the late 1960's.

The children were given the opportunity to eat a marshmallow. Ones who ate it immediately only received one marshmallow. The ones who waited for an undetermined time (up to fifteen minutes) would receive a second marshmallow.

Most of the children couldn't wait. Most grabbed and ate the first marshmallow immediately.

The psychologist tracked the participants over the next forty years. The children who waited for the second marshmallow went on to live productive, and in many cases, outstanding lives. Those who immediately grabbed a marshmallow didn't do as well.

Walter Mischel, the Stanford psychology professor who did the study, got serious about tracking the students in 1981. He studied every trait he could think of.

The students who couldn't wait were more prone to adult behavior problems and inability to deal with stress.

When they got to college age, the nursery school students who waited 15 minutes averaged SAT scores 215 points higher than those who could only wait 30 seconds.

Mischel seems to have discovered the Rosetta Stone of why some people become wealthy and others do not.

Maybe we are on to something? Could this perhaps indirectly relate to our personal and leadership development? Consider this in the quest for our calling as leaders.[1]

American philosopher Dr. Wayne Dyer once stated, "Change the way you look at things, the things you look at, change." We invite our readers—each of you—to be willing to become grateful for this statement, to enjoy its freedom, and to read these pages looking for changing the way you look at things. Your authors also pursue this in life, also partaking this same life's journey. As genuine partners with thoughts, not with answers. After all, these authors intend to serve a unique blend of responses only you can conjure up in the right moment of need.

Trust finding what works . . . your spirit always recognizes.

LEADERSHIP PRACTICES THAT HAVE WORKED—CAN THEY WORK FOR YOU?

ROLE MODEL THEORY IN USE #1

People do business with people they like. Sell the relationship first, the capabilities second.

Story One

One way this may "sound" over time comes through this perspective of a successful salesperson:

> *He never sees himself as a salesman going to the customer. He asks to understand their issues, maybe describe to them why [such and such] is important. . . . They don't hear the company's name in those things . . . they hear issues important to them, they hear this is what we've done, what we can't do, what things they should be thinking about. They eventually ask the salesperson, "Can your company [you] do this?" [and] "Can you help us here?" Otherwise, they sense when the salesperson simply selling.*

Story Two

"Bring your assets, not your agenda . . . story of a homeless person."

A good friend shared that in business we always bring our agenda, when we should bring our assets. Pondering this, the author realized he was right. When meeting new people, we bring our agenda, whether it is our business or services. We focus on what we can gain from the interaction. But how much more effective might we be if we brought our assets instead?

His illustration was in meeting a homeless person. As the reader, say to yourself, do you try to sell the homeless person a product or service? No, you have no agenda because you know that can't really help the person. Instead, you bring your assets. You focus on how you can help him. You ask if you can help them with food, or take them to a shelter, or some other way to help them.

What if we approached all of our relationships, whether personal or professional, by bringing our assets rather than our agendas?

Questions from the leader's circle:
In conversation with others, are you thinking internally, in the background, "what can you do for me?"
Or does your thinking quietly voice "what can I do for you?
What can I bring this person/this team/this organization?"
Am I thinking assets first, or agenda?
Which becomes the more effective (and more familiar) internal place from which to manifest my intentions outwardly?
To create a change in my behavior and conversation from within me?
Which calls upon my personal courage of convictions and requires my creative willingness to think on possibilities instead of a fixed end point of how things will be?

Practical application: One change in conversational response habit can interrupt the fine line between the two ends of this relationship spectrum driven by assets on the one end versus transactional agenda on the opposite end.

A "Yes, but" response becomes fueled by who is right and correct, favoring agenda. A "Yes, and" response considers the relationship moving forward as well as the agenda, promoting further productive conversation.

People do business with people they like. People talk with people who reflect their assets, hopes, and aspirations. It becomes easier to ignore a statement than to ignore a question—a question posed from a place of honest, genuine enquiry inspires others from within, even in those times when others may feel stuck and paralyzed by details, conflicting information, competing emotions.

If what we resist persists as a tendency in our human experience, perhaps genuine questions invite a response that seeks not to resist but to discover, to unveil a new way of thinking and thus a new way of acting.

Correlation: Where do you find connections to other leaders' theory in use practices here?

ROLE MODEL THEORY IN USE #2

What operating definition of leadership gets proposed and implications for personal decision and personal action manifested through one's personal behavior?

Story One

As part of a Fortune 100 global company, the author found himself included on a list of folks invited to the company headquarters location. Our CEO had been mentored by a "leadership philosopher" known to mentor CEOs around the world for a living. Introduced as Peter Koestenbaum, and appearing like a distinguished yet approachable jolly old fellow, he asked the group of us, "what is your definition of leadership?" We pretty much offered a military-style definition, such as, "The ability to influence people to act." I just knew this would not meet his expectation.

Briefly pausing and giving us eye contact, he managed to figuratively have veteran corporate leaders at the edge of their seats, anticipating his response. He replied, "I am still thinking about and learning about this thing called leadership. And so far, I have concluded, it is connecting with another human being."

Note, Peter did not claim to know, he did not definitively claim, "My [or The] definition of leadership is . . ." Simply, with confident humility, he emphasized connecting with another human being.

Since comparing and contrasting these two leadership definitions, the author discovered that both similarity and contrast indeed existed when coaching role model business leaders. They give examples of "connecting" over "influencing." Can you perceive a changed inner awareness of *what you notice* when hearing a reference to "human being" instead of to the more commonly used term "people?"

Story Two

This one particularly honors the math teachers among us!

Invited to observe a tenth grade algebra class by a teacher planning a team class activity, the author arrived early as the previous period concluded. Sitting in the back row, one noticed the teacher standing by the door, greeting students as they entered her room. Eventually, she had teams competing by calling on an individual representative of each team to explain the process of solving a joint class problem. If one team's representative miscalculated on the front whiteboard, a different team's representative could take over and explain it, acquiring points for their team.

Things were going fine, until the inevitable emotional outburst. When the teacher called on one student to give her team's solution, the student quickly blurted out, "Why are you always picking on me? I refuse to do this!" (Naturally, the teacher has an observer [the author] in the room as well when this occurs.)

Before sharing the rest of the story and this teacher's seizing carpe diem, seizing the day through her chosen response while thinking on her feet (as all good teachers do continually every school day), let us compare two sample leadership definitions and their implications for each of us here.

How would you instantaneously reply to this student had you followed an operating definition of leadership more like "influencing people to act?" Operationalizing "influencing people to act," how might I influence this student through my reply?

In contrast, how would you instantaneously respond differently to this student had you followed an operating definition of leadership closer to "connecting with another human being?" Operationalizing "connecting with another human being," how might you connect differently to this student through your response?

Finally, what might be the learning behind us contrasting the verb "reply" in the former paragraph, with the verb "response" in the latter?

Now for the rest of the story: The algebra teacher, pausing, with all eyes in the class (including the other adult set of eyes—mine) looking at her, calmly responds, "I appreciate that you are having a bad day, and I respect your choice to decline to answer."

Then she states to all sets of eyeballs on the teacher expressing, "What are you going to say now," the entire class of eyeballs hear, "We all have the occasional bad day, me included. That is one reason I stand by the door as you come into class every day. This is your opportunity to say Ms. _____, I am having a bad day, please do not call on me. And I will respect that."

Later, the teacher indicated she had talked privately with the student in question that day. Of course, the student apologized (although that does not always happen in our lives). She indicated her uncle, who she was close to, had just died the previous day. The student did not want to go to school that following day but indicated her dad required her go to school.

As you read the story, what evidence comes to mind of the operational leadership definition of this algebra teacher? The term "operational" becomes one means of signifying what we do instantaneously, thinking on our feet, especially, in the face of rising emotions.

This may generally reveal how your operating leadership definition influences real-time what a plan, what in this case a classroom lesson plan, or in your case a life's plan, cannot duplicate.

As we segue into questions from the leader's circle, note two readers' responses to this story in reflection:

I think the real secret to this teacher's success is the fact she is at the door everyday greeting her students. This teacher clearly understands the value of creating meaningful relationships with her students. I love how she remained calm when the student spoke out. She then attacked the situation with a little love and logic. She used some empathy and let the students know that it is okay to feel that way from time to time.

Talking to the student in private instead of calling the kid out was also a well-executed plan. You can tell that it was not her first time with a situation like that. I bet she also showed some more empathy when they had their talk in private. I also have a feeling that she let the student know that sometimes we are having a bad day but there is still a polite way to respond. Even when we are having a bad day we still have to do work.

What a great example of character education. Students are always watching us. I bet most of us do our best work without the lesson plans.

[and]

Thank you for sharing that wonderful story with us. As an observer, I often wonder when asked, "How are you or how is your day?" Most of the time the automatic response is, "I'm doing good or I'm doing fine." There are times when people forgo common courtesy by saying, "Hello or how are you today?" to people they encounter or provide them service. This reminds me of that student and how the teacher interacted with her. There is a recurring theme on empathy throughout your story. There is the underlying theme about honesty in the story as well. There is a feeling of lightness when you admit and become honest with yourself. It takes a certain character to encourage openness and honesty. The teacher in the story has the wisdom and kindness that deflects the negativity. Her genuine interest and care for her students shows that her students respect her. It is important how trivial to others to just acknowledge others. Because as the teacher taught us, we have no idea what others around us are going through. We need more people like her.

Questions from the leaders' circle:

Will you be counted as one of those "we need more people like her" leaders, regardless of calling or industry or profession? What defines your leadership?

How does your current definition of leadership define (guide/influence) thinking and actions as a leader while on your feet?

What personal definition of leadership inspires your courage, patience, empathy, your actions and decisions? Acknowledging variables of situation and people, does your leadership belief inform more often to serve and encourage through personal modeling, or inform to control and admonish? What pattern of inner voice reveals to you the operating definition of leadership you use?

If seeking clarity of one's personal definition of leadership, what clues can be provided by recalling your recent decisions/actions/conversations? Could they be characterized more as posturing how right and correct one's position sounds? Or characterized by my deliberative attempts to listen and understand the views of others?

Practical application: When getting stuck and uncertain as to what to say or do in a pinch, or when finding ourselves wishing later we had responded differently, one way to become unstuck may be to swim further upstream instead of downstream. Swimming further upstream to a less obvious or more subconscious operational definition of leading and of core values of leadership. A clarification of those values will perhaps reveal what is most important in any given situation, informing how one responds. To what do you aspire in each episode of day-to-day interactions with others? Does aspiration trump emotional triggers?

Correlation: What else do I think about which correlates to this discussion of identifying my primary leadership definition and its implications in my responses to others?

If perchance I regularly attend a church service, how might this discussion extend what I spiritually aspire to be, into who I am through my behaviors the remaining time outside of the church/mosque/synagogue doors?

Love and logic—at odds with you, or familiar partners in your outward manifestation toward others?

ROLE MODEL THEORY IN USE #3

More on leadership and leadership defined. In an interview for a collaborative book called *Speaking of Success*, Stephen Covey indicates that his definition of leadership *is communicating people's worth and potential so clearly that they are inspired to see it in themselves.*

Thinking back on this author's operating definition of leadership and the implications for my personal leadership behavior, could a by-product of connecting with another human being create a means of communicating that inspires others to see their worth and potential through the daily events, even working through the experience of daily problems and unfortunate circumstances?

Story One

A role model business leader recalled an instance where he sat in on a client meeting that one of his organization's leaders held. The conversation unexpectedly turned negative, as client representatives threatened to terminate the contract and rudely complained over a series of issues. Following the meeting, at one point only the two of them remained.

As they shut off the lights and walked the hallway, the role model leader broke the uneasy silence, stating, "I for one appreciate you biting your tongue in there for the last hour, and I know practicing patience is tough. But we all benefit from hearing the clients being able to vent."

Eventually walking their separate ways, the leader in charge of client relationships immediately established a plan and set in work a series of steps to repair and strengthen the relationships with those angry clients.

Story Two

A great example of understanding someone's worth is the story of King David, one of the early kings of Israel. No one thought he deserved to be king because he was too young, because he was too small, and because he had older brothers, maybe one of them should be king. If David had placed his worth in what the people around him thought, he may never have been successful, much less become king. But rather, he saw his own worth based upon the strengths and talents that God had given him.

In an interview with Miss USA International, Nova Pearson Kopp, she shared how she had to rewire her brain and thinking to realize she had worth. She was abused as a child and as the ultimate act of child abuse, her father committed suicide when she was in ninth grade.

Nova said from that point that she basically was in survival mode. She had no self-confidence or sense of worth. She married and was divorced by her early twenties and found herself alone trying to raise two children on her own making minimum wage as a receptionist.

Nova said at that point she finally realized there was more to life than barely surviving and that God had created her for a purpose beyond her current situation. From that point, she started setting big goals. Goals that could be accomplished only by someone who knew he or she had great worth and a purpose in life.

Since that time, Nova graduated college (at the age of 42) and is now an executive with ATT. She has several side businesses she has started or bout out, and she is currently Miss USA International. Now she feels that her purpose is to help others who feel like their life is hopeless and to build them up and improve their lives as well.

Nova is in every sense of the word a servant leader who knows she has a purpose greater than herself!

Questions from the leader's circle:
Referring to the time in the previous story one, what do you think the subordinate leader in charge of client relationships expected to hear from his boss, the role model leader?

Think to yourself—Had you been the leader, think about your own definition of leadership. What really would you have typically stated to one of your employees in that scenario who on the surface appeared to not measure up to his or her responsibilities? Could you hear myself communicating in the words of Covey, to a person's worth and potential so clearly, as for the employees to see it in themselves? Are you about building up or unwittingly tearing down relationships?

From story two, what is your takeaway from this? Do you see hope replace despair? How can you change the way you currently see reality as you define it? Does the universal face of leadership apply to all ages and backgrounds of human beings, all the way to King David?

Practical application: In terms of how to, in terms of one way to communicate a person's worth and potential so clearly, notice that the leaders in all three stories chose to highlight an observable feature or behavior of the employee and student and one's inner purpose that was productive.

The role model leader in the first story viewed from an expanded perspective. Notice the part about "we all benefit from hearing the clients being able to vent?" What did this suggest? Could the role model leader recognize that, even if impolitely, at least the clients were talking, were venting, were communicating?

Could the role model leader project forward into the future how this could be seen as an opportunity, rather than a dead end and reason to finger point round bazillion of the blame game? Could the middle-school teacher be projecting forward into the future young people's behaviors today?

From the story with Miss USA International, how does one measure and perhaps limit one's self worth and potential based on the thinking of colleagues/acquaintances? Or does one sense something greater and use that vision to guide life's steps one step at a time?

Correlation: How do these examples reflect your own self-talk, that inner conversation going on inside your mind?

Even though you think no one else can hear your self-talk (and they cannot unless mental telepathy was at work), do your comments and actions eventually reveal your self-talk for all to see and hear?

What about embodying and communicating a grateful mind-set reflects connecting with another human being? How does that reflection clearly communicate the worth and potential of another such that they begin to see it in themselves?

ROLE MODEL THEORY IN USE #4

A popular morning ESPN sports (naturally) TV segment called *Mike and Mike* often interviews coaches from all levels of sports and from all categories (basketball, baseball, football, etc.) of sports. (These pages later unfold an interview with Mike Singletary on leadership through his experiences.) While these coaches represent unique and individual styles and personalities, one common tendency when listening to their responses becomes their genuine interest in their players.

This interest is often driven by a desire to develop and grow. At the professional level, it may become more focused on specifically playing to a player's strengths. The human interest remains. Ever hear a coach on *Mike and Mike* or other interview segments indicate "we are who we are because of me?" In various industries, what are the hallmark clues as to how leaders "coach" their teams of employees, even when their role is not formally described as one of leader as "coach?"

Story One

This story exemplifies how a coach as dad chose to respond in a crisis and communicated taking over from his daughter in the process. Father and his daughter were flying a single engine plane over Lake Michigan, when the engine stalls with the daughter at the controls.

Dad did not state "what did you do?" He did not react with any implied dose of accusation as to the mistake the one in control must have logically caused for such a problem to occur.

Dad simply says to daughter, "Honey, I need to fly the plane differently." Her response? "You have it dad." On the second dive, as they approached the water's surface, dad was able to restart the engine.

The author (Brad) interviewed Coach Bobby Bowden for a previous educational leadership book. While he never used the term "role model," he did refer to himself as a father figure to his players.

As he explained, "Many of these boys came from broken home, or no home. They had no one to help guide or correct them. I would do my best to help students get their lives straightened out in the 4 years they were with me."

Coach Bowden said while he was the coach and in charge, he needed to "show his players and staff that I was working with them, then they are more willing to follow. You can't be a dictator. I always put the players first. Even if a student got in trouble, I would usually give them a second chance. The easiest thing to do is kick them off the team. But I felt like I needed to save these kids by giving them second chance. So, I would find ways to make them accountable rather than just kicking them off the team."

Coach Bowden was well known for his mantra, faith, family, and football. He emphasized this by having devotions with the students, taking them to church when he could, and he had an open door policy where students could share any life concerns or problems with him.

So, while he never used the term "role model" and probably didn't even see himself as one, he was a role model to his players, his staff, and thousands of fans!

Story Two

Jogging on a track, the author overheard a coach (likely a volunteer parent coaching their child's soccer team, God bless them!) yell out to the team in a practice session, "Don't kick the ball high." Role model leaders' stories about coaching focus communicating in terms of what to do, not in terms of what not to do. This recollection immediately caused this author to reframe the parent coach's encouragement into what to do, as in, "Kick the ball low!"

Questions from the leader's circle:
Question for you—when *your* engine stalls, when an unexpected, unpleasant impulse occurs, do the people who know you well hear you sound like "Honey, I need to fly the plane differently." Or do they hear something like, well, something one would not dare share and utter with this fine, distinguished group of leader readers?
Do you coach in terms of what not to do ("Don't fumble the ball")? Could the brain automatically key on or visualize the very word "fumble," on precisely what one should not do? Could then fumbling the ball become a matter of how we create our reality as coaches?
Focusing on purpose, translate into vision and goals, into what to do, not what not to do. Do we even know what to do ("Hold on to the ball")? How does one influence the performance and confidence of others?

Practical application: When someone seeks advice in a coaching scenario, two questions replace "How can I help you?/What can I do for you?" First question, "What is it you most want to have happen?" (in this conversation, or in your situation or dilemma?)

This first question works to begin to clarify purpose and intent for the requesting party. This question can begin to help the requesting person cast a warm beam of recognizing what is most important through the fog of temporary confusion.

Second question, "How can I support you?" Generally using this second question in tandem with the first question (What is it you most want to have happen?). This calls out to the assets of the requesting party. This becomes situationally important at precisely the time the requesting party may be experiencing victim mentality and unintentionally dismissing their own personal assets.

When in a coaching scenario, and oftentimes on the spur of the moment, unexpectedly, one wonders how might a series of follow-up questions in a conversation sound differently when following up the first two leading set of questions, "What is it you most want to have happen? and How can I support you?"

Are you listening and asking questions to understand, as coach? Or do you find yourself from a place of vigor, asking questions to lead and lecture? Do you ask questions more like a "what" question? What makes you do it this way? or Do you ask questions more like a "why" question? Why do you do it this way?

Which set of questions more frequently promotes more productive resolution and growth/expansion in thinking more quickly? Is time money?

"What is it you most want to have happen? How can I support you?" Two questions clarifying what is most important amid the fog of emotions, ownership, investment of personal pride, and detailed events. Two sample questions that help us coach others (and ourselves as coach) to call on our courage in the face of fear, and our values in the face of chaos and high stakes.

Correlation: Remember Brad's story about the homeless person (People do business with people they like)? Instead of becoming lost or caught up in the quicksand of details and operating from one's own prejudices, biases, likes, and dislikes—will one tend to see Christ, to see that homeless person for whom we become destined to serve with our guidance and support, rather than limited by the dictates of one's opinion?

What spells the difference for you between providing guidance and providing your opinion for anyone who feels temporarily homeless or helpless in a specific situation?

Do you ask questions that you think you already know the answer to?

Or do you find yourself asking questions from a true sense of curiosity and wonder at what responses they may evoke?

ROLE MODEL THEORY IN USE #5

Switching one's focus or preoccupation *from* what is not working *toward* what is working.

Story One

In our conversations with teachers across the globe in a graduate program, many often observe our tendency to key on the negative, on what is not working, on the problem behavior of specific people. We then begin a path to experience a new reality. This occurs when acknowledging it requires awareness and admission to make a change through repeated conscious choice.

This point reminds this author of the pattern of business role model leader responses to the question, "What do you say or do to create such role model perception ratings from your employees across [leadership] behaviors?"

In one particular scenario involving extremes, one leader had replaced a leader whose team suffered from low morale, hated their boss, hated their jobs, hated each other! One year later, I found myself seated again with this new leader, noting her role model markings from these same employees across a series of leadership behaviors comprising a leadership performance feedback survey.

She was asked, "Can you point to one thing you did that most created this turnaround among perception and attitudes of your employees?" [Be thinking here, of the worst class of students in the school!] "Yes," she replied. "In a customer satisfaction review, my team used to focus on the 2 percent we did not do or get right. I have since coached them now on focusing first on the 98 percent we did get right. As a result, you can see the release of power and energy from within."

This last phrase suggests something very powerful, or as Disney leadership might suggest, very magical.

Other role model leaders often cited giving feedback on what to do, as opposed on what not to do. For example, "Hold on to the ball" instead of "Don't fumble the ball." One possible classroom translation might be "Remain quiet," instead of "Don't talk." The brain hears fumble, or talk and the next thing you know the player fumbles the ball or the student talks!

The coach stands on the sidelines shouting, "What more could I have done, I told you 'Don't fumble' and you did!" Little do we know that we placed that undesired image in their mind. We can influence our reality. It starts with awareness, as teachers so wisely point out.

This awareness becomes exemplified in this next story. The author was observing a student teacher who was giving directions for her first grade students as they were transitioning into their reading groups. She told the students to make sure they "stay on task."

She continued to share her expectations when one of the students raised his hand and asked, "What do you mean to stay on task?" So, she explained in more detail and in terms the student better understood. To which he replied, "Ok, I understand now."

This was a teachable moment for the students and even the student teacher. In fact, it was the focus of our post-observation discussion.

We can have high expectations of students or employees, but those expectations need to be communicated clearly and with understanding, in order to communicate meaning and a mutual response from those we lead.

Story Two

As one exception to strict storytelling, a potential personal developmental bridge to closing the gap between focusing on what works versus what is not working keys on Dr. Carol Dweck's theory of communicating in terms of the power of yet. Specifically, in place of telling a child or adult they are failing, one replaces failing with "Not yet."

The overall focus shifts from one of a fixed mind-set valuing who we are based on what we know, and measuring intelligence limited by a personal status quo, to one of growth, of our ability to grow and develop over time fed by our perseverance and effort. Overall, this reminds us of earlier lessons in the 1990s, when we heard about the joy of focusing more on process and journey, and less on the end game or destination.

More can be readily gleaned from viewing Carol's work through YouTube presentations.

Story Three: Stuck versus Unstuck

This story transfers a glimpse of martial arts into this thread of intentionally shifting our focus from what is not working to what is working in order to expand our capacity for action both in ourselves and among those around us.

A person had been experiencing troubles rooted in a feeling of being stuck. Always experiencing the same inevitable feelings of despair and helplessness over time, as predictable as the seasons. She then experienced significant health problems, further compounding her frustration and experience. She sought the wisdom of a master in martial arts.

He applied a hold on her, and requested she break free of the hold. She tried, and failed.

Releasing the hold, the master asked her to reflect on her thoughts as she recalled them while attempting to break free from the hold. She recalled "I can't move (this), I can't do (that)."

The master asked her, "Where was your mind preoccupied?" She realized her mind felt trapped by what she could not do, by her circumstances.

The master asked her, "Where else could your mind focus?" Thinking about it, she replied, "On where I am free to move?"

As one can predict, the master reapplied the same hold. Intentionally thinking only about where she could move, she found the ability to make movements among fingers, elbows, and eventually, she figured a way to break free of the hold.

Similar to Carol Dweck's focus on the power of yet, and similar to the role model leaders' focus on what to do over what not to do, on what we are getting right, this leads us to some questions and potential application, potential replacement of old habits with new habits of thinking leading to new ways of behaving and experiencing a leader's reality.

Questions from the leader's circle:
When you hear the reference leaders make who cite their success to surrounding themselves with good people as one fundamental strategy, how could the theory in use of focusing on what is working help me create the goodness among those people already surrounding me (already a part of my team, my family, my extended network)?
How may it further extend people's strengths naturally in what gets accomplished?

Practical application: (1) Be mindful of how we think, then talk . . . do we encourage in terms of what to do (Hold on to the ball) or in terms of what not to do (Don't fumble the ball)? (2) Recognize others for the intangibles and for process ("I for one appreciate you biting your tongue . . . practicing patience enabled the clients to vent") more so than the tangibles and results ("You won this round with the clients/signed that contract.")

Correlation: How does this tie into flying the plane differently when your engine stalls?

ROLE MODEL THEORY IN USE #6

See the connectedness of otherwise disparate events, as evidenced through the brush strokes of visionary leaders or strategic thinkers.

Story One

Years ago (approximately the late 1990s), a former biologist turned leadership consultant, Margaret Wheatley, spoke about something she called chaos theory and its application in our lives. She spoke about how scientists observed patterns of order emerge out of the chaos when observing nature, whether at the smallest quantum level or the larger Newtonian level.

This author became awed by her own stories and the implications revealing the recognition of patterns unique to teams and systems. This recognition can be applied to our own ways to either expand or contract our future through our own actions and beliefs. It supports the oft-stated notion that believing big becomes a gateway to eventual big things.

In particular, the author recalls Margaret noting that nature and life seeks what works, not what is the perfect solution. This question was posed. "How much time, energy, certainty do we invest, if it is not perfect, we do not want our names attached?"

While those of us with perfectionistic tendencies can think about this, immediate focus here becomes how recognition of chaos theory and patterns of order emerging out of the chaos can fuel one's resolve to enjoy the journey and be committed for the long run as leaders. This leads to the following personal story.

Story Two

In the months following my personal reflection on Margaret's presentation to chaos theory, I experienced the unexpected. Chaos theory teased my awareness as it became illustrated by a sixth grade special needs student. I attended an overnight as part of a week-long camping experience for my daughter's school. I followed along as my daughter's class attended to a deep-woods excursion for a series of activities. One had to admire observing how some of the sixth graders volunteered to attend to a special needs classmate.

At one location, our guides informed the class they needed to break down into pairs. Grunts and groans became followed by students explaining to the special needs student referring to me as a dad/adult, meaning he could not pair up with me. Sensing this I quickly indicated my pleasure to pair up with the student.

Instructions directed that each pair had to walk a short distance to spread out from the other pairs. Then one member asked a series of given questions printed on a 3×5 card for the partner to answer.

First prompt stated, "Find something here, and pick it up." My partner picked up a maple leaf from the ground.

The next question: "What do you see?" He replied in a voice one could discern, "A leaf." The next question: "Look deeper at this same object, and tell me what you see?" My student partner quickly and simply replied, "A tree."

Looking in astonishment, indeed, the perfect image of a maple tree was outlined in the leaf (the kind of maple tree with a shape which would cause you the reader to want it gracefully overlooking your yard). Indeed, the veins of every leaf displayed this same perfect image of a tree.

This revealed a glimpse into the chaos theory as presented by Margaret Wheatley. Revealed by a sixth grade special needs student who otherwise had no benefit of previously hearing her presentation.

I myself had not been looking for chaos theory, but my partner showed me. Some smart ones among us could readily dismiss an application of this to which a very young person can see through a child-like lens.

Story Three

Always mindful of this quote attributed to Mother Teresa, "I am not called to be successful. I am called to be faithful," a scenario akin to Paul Harvey's "the rest of the story" follows. Recalling a news article, it proposed the premise that a news reporter, interviewing Mother Teresa, finally asked, [paraphrased from memory] "What makes you think you can eradicate the plight of the poor, when entire countries and whole organizations have tried and failed?" To which Mother Teresa simply and profoundly responded, "I am not called to be successful. I am called to be faithful."

Story Four: The Prodigal Son

In the New Testament, Gospel of Luke, chapter 19, Jesus shares the story of the prodigal son. This son had requested and received his share of the estate, and proceeded to depart and squander it. He returned to his father requesting he be allowed to return as a hired hand.

Instead, the father welcomed him with a party and a feast of his fattened calf. The older son became angry and told his father how he had never left and yet never received a party. But now his brother returns to this.

His father reminded his son that all that is the father's would be his, but to celebrate the one who was considered lost and dead has been found.

Questions from the leader's circle:
If a sixth grader can readily identify chaos theory while not knowing the language of chaos theory, what do we need to help us recognize the systems view within which we operate?
Do we recognize those times when we hold on too tightly, in order to make a decision with enough information even if not all the information?
Can people paralyze others through their subconscious analysis paralysis, getting teams of people stuck in unnecessary details?
Do you define your reactions limited to the sting of the past or allow my vision for the larger picture to inform my response, to prevent rigidity from seizing up any options?

To which do we tend to favor . . . being successful, or being faithful? Which prevents us from loosening our grip so that information and systems can flow freely?

To which do you prefer to be called—to be successful, or to be faithful? Which calling gives you more promise, more leverage, in the drama of any moment, of any occasion?

Practical application: Whether through feedback from a 360 degree leadership survey, or other feedback resource, determine if when delegating I am perceived as holding on, or able to let go of how employees achieve results.

Correlation: How do these four stories overlap? What does chaos theory, being faithful over being successful, avoiding the temptation of a grudge to welcome one who learned a life's lesson, and the sixth grader's recognition of patterns—what do these four stories reveal to me? What new ways of responding come to mind?

Thinking about the last question, hear how these stories influenced one classroom teacher over time, as she shared with me:

> *Now, as I enter the fourth quarter of my first year, I look at it a little differently. Instead of being upset that 20% (one out of five) of my students aren't following along with the lesson, I am grateful that I still have the attention of 80% of my class.*
>
> *I have begun not focusing so much on the negative behaviors of my students, but rather applauding the ones who are on task. Through this I am not losing anyone else's attention, and as long as those 20% are not being disruptive and are still getting their work done, I let them stray off onto their own course. Students will never learn how to stand on their own two feet if we do not start to let them find their independence.*

Pretty powerful example of love and logic, might one think?

ROLE MODEL THEORY IN USE #7

More habits and techniques from the leaders rated as visionary by their employees and peers in survey feedback.

Story One

Leaders rated as model visionaries or strategic thinkers shared patterns of similar responses when I asked them how they come across as visionary, as leaders who promote productive debate and discussion, who promote creative, out-of-the-box thinking that results in business improvements,

Patterns of responses included asking a "what" and a "how" question more often than a "why" question (question starting with the word why). For example, someone states to you, "This situation is helpless." You state "why do you say that?" Role model leaders indicate that the more probable (generic) response is a more emotional, "They're jerks, that's why."

Instead, asking "what makes you say that?" promotes a higher chance for a more objective, less emotional response, such as "well, it's [this and that]." In turn, this more quickly promotes a more constructive, productive, and less destructive conversation.

Another technique often cited entailed asking the same question in a different way. For a generic example, consider a multiple-choice question: What's the right answer, (a), (b), or (c)? A way to ask that question differently: In what situations might (a) be the better answer? When might (b) or (c) be the better solution?

Multiple-choice questions are good questions. The distinction leaders make becomes noting the difference between asking multiple-choice questions as a rule and switching to asking that same question differently as you recognize the need and your intentions.

Story Two

When brainstorming, leaders with visionary tendencies recognize a process of asking questions that intentionally create a divergence of answers and responses. At some point, they sense when to switch over to a series of questions that then help participants to converge.

One example of how this transition from diverging to converging may sound is "What do we now know we did not realize when we began this conversation?"

Story Three

Leaders with visionary tendencies recognize the power of a visual diagram or illustration to help free people's thinking when seeking a clearer understanding of the issue, resolution, or goal. Further, some indicate they cannot draw worth a darn! What then? They recognize there are natural drawers with some artistic capability in every group.

Story Four

Leaders with visionary tendencies recognize the power of—all things—sharing stories. Again, the intention may be to clarify shared values or to help people become unstuck.

In the latter case of a group appearing to be stuck, the leader may ask, "Does this remind anyone of a situation you have been in from the past?"

Usually someone shares a story, and the effect of that process begins to create a space for people to think more freely.

Story Five

Leaders with visionary tendencies value the use of humor to loosen people's thinking and gain a free flow of ideas among the group. Again, leaders recognize not everyone is a comedian. However, there are inspired comedians in almost every moment waiting for an invitation in the meeting.

The author has noted how speaker/evangelizer Joel Osteen begins each program with a joke. While thinking about a purpose, one wonders if an intention could serve to free people's thinking in preparation for the message he is about to share. Many presenters integrate humor into their messages.

Questions from the leader's circle:
Which of these stories reminds me of me?
Do most of them? Do any of them?
Do you identify these stories as habits of individuals you know? If so, could you seek them as mentors or coaches to further develop my comfort with promoting a group thinking more strategically, thus making more informed decisions?
If you tend to be more operational oriented in my life's experience, how could recognizing these behaviors help me support those who attempt the balance of a strategic mind-set?

Practical application: Find a safe group and scenario in which to either practice these techniques or to discuss them. This may promote your personal balance of tactical, more immediate, near-term orientation with a more strategic, long-term orientation.

Together, this may both strengthen my tactical strength and further develop my strategic thinking.

Correlation: How do these practices further strengthen relationships through conversations? How might adding the practices of the visionary, strategic thinkers, as a new normal, contribute to my team experiencing a decided, competitive advantage?

ROLE MODEL THEORY IN USE #8

What the author discovers as a secondary school's consultant/literacy coach about correlation of classroom experiences with leadership, weaves through these next two theories in use.

Story One

Before these years in education, the author served in the corporate world. One summer afternoon conversation in the corporate offices mentioned a "woe is me" dialogue suggesting how nice it would be to work as a teacher. After all, they do get the entire summer off.

This demonstrates potential blindness, not knowing what one does not know. One of the chief discoveries for this consultant literacy coach in various middle and high schools over the years is that teachers are usually overworked and underpaid . . . the summer is not long enough! Appreciation and gratitude for what our teachers do warrants this initial shout out to all our educators at all levels.

Story Two

Experiencing a first-ever interview with a team of educators, one's drive to the location combines anxiety and excitement. Anxiety, because one had not been in academic education before, and understood to some extent that one knew what was unknown.

Excitement, because one experienced facilitating corporate adult leadership courses, alongside a host of other lifetime experiences we each accumulate. One just sensed there would be something new to apply all of this and grow.

I caught a glimpse of four educators in the conference room, waiting to interview me. One of "them" exited the room to greet me in this way: "Remember one thing. We are not here to figure out if we want you. We are here for you to figure out if you want us. Ask as many questions as you like."

Hearing this, one thought sounded like this: "Wow, in this day and age of procedural rules in business, I never thought I would experience what my grandfather and grandmother might have experienced in their day . . . a hiring decision made over a shake of the hand instead of signing various forms, and where you peed in a cup not for a drug test, but after enjoying some adult beverages as you became acquainted."

Obviously, there were no adult beverages in this episode associated with the hiring interview; this was all done proper and yet special, as if in the old days, if you catch the drift.

Questions from the leader's circle:

What if you told a candidate for the job, just prior to the team interview, "We are here for you to figure out if you want us?" How would this changing of a conversational paradigm between potential employer and employee from one of "what can you do for me?" to "what can we do for you?" influence the type of future employees?

What could you learn about a prospective employee from this changing of the interview chairs? What might this suggest about your company's culture? How might this influence employee attitudes toward your clients or customers across any industry?

What becomes the character of your people, the character of your organization's core, through the conduct of your first impressions?

Practical application: Taking a look at "standard" procedures—yours, or that of your organization. How might seeking one area to flip potentially grow one's capacity through increased choices?

Correlation: How does the interview experience, reversing roles as stated by the lead interviewer, promote Covey's leadership of communicating people's worth so clearly, they are inspired to see it in themselves?

ROLE MODEL THEORY IN USE #9

More discoveries as a secondary school consultant/literacy coach.

Context to the following stories: One of the goals as a literacy coach in classrooms grades 5–12 entailed reaching out to alliterate readers. Not readers who could not read (illiterate), nor readers who did read (literate), but those readers who could read but refused to read (alliterate). Students heard me introduced as an author with a business background.

We would first talk about the difference between reading narrative and reading informational writing. I would often invite students to project into a future after school, asking them, What kind of books do mechanics refer to? Do doctors? What surrounds lawyers in their office? And how did these reference manuals appear—small, or typically large (usually showing them their textbook as an example).

We would then talk about how professionals—blue and white collar, across industries and callings—read these manuals . . . not by reading from beginning to end (as a narrative might usually be read). Rather, the reader for an informational reading typically scanned for the key information they needed at the time (for a specific brake procedure, a specific case ruling, a medical proceeding).

Students each received a copy of a high-interest reading, and I guided them with prompts as they then highlighted key information. At this juncture, I would give them a timed (sixty seconds or so) opportunity to review what they had highlighted as well as the entire article. They then took a brief, timed multiple-choice quiz.

Once we discussed the results and how this experience (of skimming and scanning for key information) surprised them, we culminated my presentation by each of us writing a summary of the article we had highlighted. What ideas may this give you when communicating with these same "kids" now turned adults, in your workforce?

Story One

Here is where we pick up—the writing summary. After all, that for alliterate readers, readers who can read and do not read, does it not then follow that as writers they can write but do not write? The author often interacted with students in low-socioeconomic schools, from mainstream classrooms, to honors classrooms, to special education classrooms. This next particular sequence of events exemplified some these experiences.

After we had concluded the quiz, I would customarily challenge the class in this way. Each of us had a blank sheet and a pencil. At the sound of the teacher's "Begin" or "Go!" we had 100 seconds, timed by the teacher, to write as much as we could about the article we had skimmed and scanned through highlighting and reviewing.

The catch? Since I was the one professional author paid for my writing in the classroom, naturally I would write more words than any other student in the room (usually choosing the hands-on-hips body posture to reinforce the obvious nature of my pretentiously haughty "I need to be knocked down a notch or two" demeanor). But if one student wrote more than me, and all students wrote a minimum number of words (usually twenty-five or thirty-five), then this professional author would attempt 100 pushups in one minute, again, "timed by your teacher."

Various patterns of results would occur here. The norm was that at the sound of "Stop!" we each counted our total words, and I would ask for a show of hands, how many wrote more than forty words, fifty words, and so on. This gave the teacher immediate feedback as to how the students were doing.

When a student or (more rarely) students (plural) actually exceeded my total number of words, we then asked the top vote getter to read theirs out loud, followed by my reading mine out loud. Personally, I was amazed at how the quality of writing, of the message, of those students only attempting to "beat the author" by writing more words than me.

This brings to bear evidence confronting a belief that increased quantity means decreased quality (or that increased focus on quality suggests a decrease in quantity). Indeed, I always noted an increase in quality (or at least a retention of quality) with increased quantity. So did the kids, and the teacher.

Story Two

What happened when none of the students in the classroom beat this author in a summary writing, total number of words? At this point, students with the top two word counts were asked to read theirs out loud. I would then read mine. If the class voted on their peers having the better, more interesting summary, then I would still attempt the 100 pushups in sixty seconds.

As a reader, do you wish to make a prediction of how often the class voted on the students as having a better summary (based on certain criteria that I provided through a rubric)?

Mine was never voted as the better one. Usually, one agreed with the students. However, it was the students who one could tell were intrigued by the quality of the summary written between one and two minutes. Ask them— "Can you sense the flow, readily see the logic?" Students were alerted that by linking a personal experience into the reading, it readily became their own summary. In what ways can you add ownership to your employees' experience?

Story Three

In one particular special needs classroom, the teacher had to leave for a couple minutes. Five students were asked if they were juniors or seniors. One of the students asked, "What is a junior? What does that mean?" Reading the faces of his peers, one automatically sensed this was a genuine response. He calculated he was 11th grade equivalent, and suggested "I must be a junior then."

When the teacher returned, we began the guided highlighted reading for key information. At first, one thought this student would be unable to highlight the key information following the prompts one used. However, just as one thought of assisting him after a delay, he would eventually locate the information—accurately.

When we completed the writing summaries and the group read samples of their work, the teacher came to tears. She told this author later that she had been with these students for years, and did not see the ability that they showed that hour. As a testament to her, it was being nourished all this time, waiting for the right moment to surprise her.

Lucky for this author, one became an unwitting participant in one of the memorable hours from this teacher's career. How can meeting an employee where they are at serve both as a personal demonstration of faith in another and lead to a breakthrough for the employee? A breakthrough even for you?

Story Four

What happened when one of the students wore a cast temporarily preventing them from writing?

Situations such as this one enabled the student to become the time keeper and the teacher to also participate in writing a summary. One can tell the impact on students when teachers actually work alongside the students as a learning partner. The teacher always gave me a run for my money in terms of total words, although on occasion the opposite might occur.

Reading the summary would indicate to me a teacher ingrained with writing a final draft version on his or her first draft.

Story Five

Did the author always do the 100 pushups in one minute?

Some days required presenting in up to five different classrooms. Having to do 500 pushups seems a bit much, until you factor in over the space of a school day. One did manage to do the pushups.

And yes, sometimes one or two kids naturally challenged alongside, adding to the spectacle. Imagine an hour filled with skimming and scanning for key information, taking a quiz, writing a summary, and counting people attempting 100 pushups in under one minute.

However, one day the author decided to get cute about the process. Never a good idea. I had noted a solid, wooden table in front of a science/astronomy class. I attempted the pushups there, reasoning that all the kids could readily view and count. My hands rested on the edge of either side, with fingers slightly curled over. Only making it to eighty-two pushups, one then learned that hands totally flattened did matter as a part of technique.

But one learns something more. One suddenly heard applause. The entire class simply applauded the effort. I do not previously recall being applauded for completing 100 pushups.

Yet, applause for not completing? This reflects in that student classroom an appreciation for effort as well among our youth, per Dr. Carol Dweck's theory of communicating in terms of the power of yet (see theory in use #5).

Questions from the leader's circle:
In the context to the preceding stories, briefly highlighted featured a high-interest reading along with a guided-highlighted skimming and scanning for key information activity to reach kids who can read but refuse to read (alliterate, not illiterate readers).
Could this thinking of "applying high-interest" into the reality of an alliterate reader transfer over to the worker who can work but refuses to work? If not due to ability but to willingness, could there be some way to discover the

passion and strengths of an employee, what tickles and generates interest, to change the employee's output?

How does a sense of friendly and productive competition change the playing field for your team, your work group, your class? How does a sense of timing and use of the "clock" add a sense of applied focus and energy among my employees/students/players? How might this impact the relationships among a team? Could this clock contribute to a sense of team interaction?

What happens to a team member's perspective when one switches roles, and places the team member in your chair, behind your figurative desk? As you reverse roles, how might this influence—possibly accelerate—an expanded appreciation in perspective among others, and ultimately, yourself as well?

Thinking of story five, what might celebrating that we tried and failed draw from a team of individuals? How does being faithful over successful suggested by Mother Teresa and the power of yet suggested by Carol Dweck apply to you and how to figuratively communicate Covey's leadership perspective, communicating a person's worth and potential so clearly, as for others to see it in themselves?

Practical application: Think of language you can use that may further support my connecting to other human beings, to use Peter Koestenbaum's perspective on leadership.

In the heat of trial and error, of ongoing edits and practice, could you replace "You failed this" or "You did not do" to "You are in the process of learning," or "Not yet, keep trying and adjust accordingly."

Can you replace my "Yes, but" with "Yes, and?"

Correlation: To most of the stories describing leader's theory in use throughout this reading.

ROLE MODEL THEORY IN USE #10

The impact and awareness of my body language.

Story One

When listening to leaders rated as role models for motivation behaviors, two patterns of response to "How do I do it?" tied to their non-verbals. First, smile versus frown. Motivator role model leaders indicate they often hear feedback that they wear a smile or positive expression on their face. This invites people sharing ideas, sharing their thinking, leading to breakthroughs.

Leaders indicate that a perpetual frowner maintains energy focused on problems and issues, not on relationships and energy that promotes creative thinking and ideas to get teams to relax the grip of the past. Frowning tends to foster negative energy and emotion that delays reaching productive conclusions.

One leader told me that taking ourselves too seriously suggests a function of valuing the task. Taking ourselves less seriously becomes a function of valuing the relationship, more time with people, more ideas. Another leader asks herself over time, "Am I still wearing the last bad expression on my face?"

Story Two

Sitting next to people in the workplace. Leaders often cited a natural tendency to sit next to people, or otherwise, to position themselves in a naturally lateral or down-at-their-level stance. One example shows a leader sitting next to a person in the workplace for even a brief conversation as opposed to standing over the seated employee.

Kneeling down to a child's level to talk and listen to the child demonstrates this second-nature awareness of leaders rated as role models for being motivational and even inspirational in the work place setting.

One leader known for not being motivational based on his feedback data from his employees objected, stating he always sits when talking to his employees at their space. Upon further enquiry, this man carrying a large frame sat on the employees' desks when talking to them, not an adjacent chair. You be the judge.

Story Three

Does this awareness of our nonverbal behavior impact integrity and other aspects of leadership seemingly removed and disparate in association? In Ohio, this author once shard feedback to a leader about sitting next to people in the workplace. He was considering changes he could make to his behavior to create more productive personal leadership.

Two days later required a return to the same building, to share tabulated and summarized feedback with yet another leader—feedback offered confidentially by the leader's employees, peers, and leader/boss.

At the precise instance the author shared with her this role model motivator pattern of feedback entailing sitting next to people when talking, she suddenly moved back and forth excitedly in her own chair and said, "I know that works!" To my "How do you know?" she replied, "My boss did that for the first time yesterday with me."

"Really?"

"Yes, and you know what?"

"What?"

"For the first time, I felt like he was genuinely listening to me, and not just pretending."

"Do you mind telling me the name of your boss?"

And indeed she replied with the name of the leader I had shared feedback with two days preceding. He was a manager, and she was one of his supervisors.

Story Four

As a literacy coach, standing in front of a class of high school juniors, the author waited to be introduced. Reading handouts to use in the upcoming reading, writing and thinking activity were already distributed to each student. To one's surprise, a whole class of students along with their teacher then entered and filled in any remaining open seats.

Since I had then given away my own copy of the handout after using all remaining copies to ensure each student had one, I knelt down beside a student seated in the first desk of the row nearest to me. I asked him, "Do I have your permission to borrow your copy so I can get us all started, and I promise to return yours to you in time?" The student nodded yes and handed me his copy.

I recalled later noticing the teachers in the back of the room suddenly whispering, one to another. One of the teachers began to approach, then stopped. As I learned later, the new students represented a special needs class joining the one already in session to sit in on my presentation.

The one teacher was whispering her alarm to another teacher at what the presenter was doing with this student and then began to approach. Apparently, the student asked to borrow a handout from was known to react violently to especially adult strangers when approached about anything.

Story Five

Story five indicates satisfied customer feedback, in the form of sample appreciation from adult students reflecting on the strictly written language provided by their professor throughout the length of an online course in graduate work:

Professor is my new best friend. I think he gave very meaningful feedback and took the time to individualize his comments to each of his students. He presents everything in a positive and helpful manner that is both respectful and professional. I feel like we've known each other much longer than the short 5 weeks of this class.

Instructor was incredibly helpful, giving constructive comments to help me improve on my mistakes so I didn't repeat them. He was also very understanding of the insanity of my current work situation. Everybody can always improve, but for me, he was fantastic.

Professor is a great instructor that encourages and gives great constructive criticism when it comes to improvement of your writing.

Looking deeper into what the three individuals separately state, what does responding in a positive manner, whether online or verbally, indicate about establishing trusting relationships with customers, employees, and other stakeholders?

Questions from the leader's circle:

Regarding story one, when you ask people around you who know you well, "Do I typically wear a frown or a smile on my face?" what pattern of response do you hear reflected back?

Regarding story four, what about awareness of body language becomes either counter-productive or productive to a conversation? Was one merely lucky that the student in question from whom the presenter borrowed his copy did not react with aggression, but simply calmly? How can my awareness of body language influence my reality?

Practical application: A question to keep as a guide, not to necessarily answer one time and discard, but to occasionally return to for a sanity check, is for me to ask myself, "Am I still wearing the last bad expression on my face?"

What becomes one nonverbal practice one can adopt to see how it influences my reality, my relationships, my own frame of mind?

Correlation: How does my nonverbal behavior support or enhance the discussion around my operating definition of leadership presented in "Theory in Use #2"?

ROLE MODEL THEORY IN USE #11

Regardless of your personal style, recognizing your people and adapting accordingly.

Story One

My first job ever, I began to work as a teenager for a German-born owner of a nursery and garden center. He had always employed a helper, and his previous one was drafted.

Joe had fought on Germany's side in World War I, immigrated to America between the world wars, and he and his wife could never bear kids. He fit the profile of a burly, tough talking, tempered man who let you know what he thought.

My first day on the job, Joe showed this author how to drive his farm tractor. We then went toward the back of his property, where one learned to dig some plants, burlap the roots, and set then on a trailer hitched to the tractor. The route to the front where the plants were to be displayed for the customer to pick up was straddled by two ponds with a dirt trail between them.

At the last second, I decided to take the middle trial instead of the trail to one side of the ponds. The front wheels caught the slope downward, and in to the water one went, tractor and all. You could see one sitting at the water's surface, and the tailpipe of the tractor protruding above the surface.

Joe immediately ran (never saw him run before or after) and went into the water, only concerned that the youthful tractor driver was alright. (This teen knew how to swim, and later found out he did not know.) Once on shore, Joe called the adjacent neighbor farmer who arrived with his tractor and, with a chain, pulled Joe's tractor out of the pond.

It took Joe a week of tinkering with the tractor in an effort to get it to start again. The author happened to be there the following weekend when he managed to start it successfully. Now, in my mind I should have been let go. Instead, what do you think this man said as soon as the tractor started up again? "Here she is. Get on."

Not once had Joe ever lecture about what one did wrong (using only the clutch to try and stop and forgetting to engage the brake stops). Not once did he threaten me, "You're fired if one more time". . . . Not once did he raise his voice (for a man who naturally and readily could raise his voice.) For the huge frame and naturally deep loud—yet with no formal leadership development, he sounded gently the entire time . . . Here's a guy who could really come across hard definitive, . . . instead. . .

In 1997, the USS *Benfold* had a change in leadership and a new captain, Mike Abrashoff, was to take over as commander of the ship. His first experience was the reception aboard the ship to bid the former captain farewell. The crew seemed glad and relieved that the former captain was leaving.

It turns out that the former captain was a very intelligent man but made the crew feel inferior and was condescending to them, which negatively affected the culture of the ship. The ship's performance was ranked last in the fleet, and the crew didn't feel safe should they be called into action.

Abrashoff recalled, "As I watched the ceremony that day and the reaction of the crew, I wondered to myself how the crew would react when I leave the ship after my tenure as captain?" He said that this thought put things into perspective quickly for him. He knew his goal was to focus on improving the morale of the crew. He said at this point in his career, other than sinking the ship, he was set as far as retirement and even advancing in rank, so his goal wasn't to use the appointment to simply advance. Instead, he wanted to make a real difference in the crew of this ship.

Over the course of his tenor as captain, Abrashoff implemented many strategies that helped build a positive culture. For instance, he created an environment where crew felt safe to take risks and take ownership in the crew's success.

As Abrashoff replied, "I took responsibility for the actions of the crew, so they knew I had their back, even if they failed." Captain Abrashoff would also publicly praise the crew when they did good work; in fact the crew affectionately named him "Mega Mike" because he would constantly praise his crew, which improved morale.

Sounding as much like a college coach as a ship captain, he said the reason that he felt like he needed to focus on the crew was that he wanted the parents of these young soldiers to be proud that their children were under his leadership.

So, he didn't see them just as a crew, but he got to know them personally and find out their interest and their strengths, so he could best utilize their talents aboard the ship. Over the course of approximately two years, Abrashoff so profoundly changed the culture of the *USS* Benfold that it went from being the worst ship in the navy to the best ship in the fleet.

Questions from the leader's circle:
What impressionistic series of leadership lessons do you think the author
    learned from this man who could speak German better than English?
How does this model and influence future leaders' ability to recognize when
    to adapt personal style to the situation—moving forward?

Practical application: Author and psychotherapist Sheldon Kopp once stated, "It's not a matter of moderation. It takes one kind of courage to wait patiently, another to get on with it."

What is the patience you call upon to interact and dance with the diverse artistry of those in your life—your family life, your business life, your personal life?

Correlation: How does the message of chaos theory and life that seeks what works, not what is the perfect solution, from Margaret Wheatley, relate to these stories?

ROLE MODEL THEORY IN USE #12

Conflict resolution. Austrian-born author and educator Riane Eisler once stated, "There will always be conflict in human affairs because of the simple fact that I'm hungry when you're thirsty, I want to sleep when you want to get up, I want to go left when you want to go right. The issue isn't conflict itself, but how we deal with it."

We are born beautifully similar and different. How we deal with conflict, the way that we choose to respond to others when we feel angst, provides us opportunities for our finest moments of leadership and humanity, regardless of our role in life.

Part of conflict resolution resides within the larger domain of how we nurture relationships with the people around us. Establishing emotional bonds through relationships at work and in the classroom contributes to a leader who contributes to a "fear-less" environment in which human beings replace intimidation with courage and a focus to perform.

The objective nature of conversations modeled by the leader during moments of breakdown fosters a performance-based and results-based culture. This leader could be called by any term across industries, such as school principal, district superintendent, manufacturing plant manager, bank branch president, classroom instructional leader, and team or shift supervisor.

Practical application: Clues as to the nature of productive conversations contributed to by leaders?

Role model leaders rated high for building good working relationships based on mutual respect and maturity often cite that ensuring conversations with colleagues are not limited to purely problem or issue-centric exchanges.

Integrating the dreams of people, always appreciating the strengths people show in the process of doing, constantly being aware of something more than just what exists on the surface in any moment, and talking in terms of what to do, and not what not to do, headline some of these clues.

As detailed in role model theory in use #5, replacing "what's right?" and "what's wrong?" with "what's working?" and "what's not working?" inspires a tendency for more productive, less blame-seeking, and fewer pointing of fingers. This naturally extends the dysfunctional emotions existing in the moment of reacting.

"What's working about this?" invites exploration through a relaxing of one's peripheral view, such that one may experience increased possibility to see and try something different, something new, some modification of previous go-to habit.

Discussion for doing so: Maslow's Hierarchy is a hierarchy for a reason.
Leaders less aware can unintentionally contribute to people existing in the bottom rung of survival more commonly by referring to right versus wrong, typically accompanied by a tone that reinforces the severity of the message and ripples throughout the organization's collective voice.

To promote increased opportunities for employees and students of any educational background to more commonly experience Maslow's top line levels of self-esteem and self-actualization becomes a function of conscious word choices and language used in everyday conversation by the leader. This especially includes conversations in a day characterized by higher tension.

Role model responses to conversations with increased tension typically referred to keeping a bigger picture in mind and recognizing the value of being in the moment by briefly yet intentionally incorporating a pause into their response. This pause often made the difference between reacting and responding.

This tendency to replace reacting with responding nurtured and strengthened relationships over time. Eventually, leaders indicate an internal question that answered temptation with a decision as to what is more important moving forward.

The question: "Is (doing, saying) this worth losing the relationship moving forward?" Questions such as these often enlightened a leader's path similarly to the biblical description of being guided like by a lantern at my feet.

Back to the pause, you ask? In the moment, when hearing anything real or perceived as unfair or even insulting directed toward you, leaders often recognized the value of adding a brief second in their response to determine other options to pursue aside from a simple reaction.

If you hear "You are a jerk!" one could reply before the "k" sound of jerk quieted, "So are you!" Leaders often cited an individual phrase one could even incorporate into the first half of your response, buying time—buying our powerful brains enough time to determine a possibly more productive and honorable reply.

Perhaps the first half might sound like, "When I hear you tell me 'I'm a jerk,' I feel the tension rising within me." (Yes, and be truthful while buying time.) Now for a possible second half to your reply. "Yet I know your heart is in the right place. What makes you refer to me as a jerk?"

More discussion: I first heard noted author, speaker, and coach Jack Canfield make this observation: $E + R = O$. Borrowing from our mathematical language, Events (E) plus our Response (R) equals (or influences) our Outcome experienced (O).

While other possibilities exist to promote productive relationships, this notion that we can influence our own reality, our own experience, by how we choose to live, to speak, and to respond, reflects our experience. When we tend to talk in terms of what to do, we keep ourselves and others focused on the possibilities, on creating resolutions.

However, when we tend to talk in terms of what not to do, in terms of the negative, do we not more frequently experience that negative outcome? Signs such as depression and dependence on substances or on others can reveal insight to our questions.

Questions from the leader's circle:
Does forgiveness play a part in relationships? How does true forgiveness do more for you than for the person or people forgiven? How does it free you to move forward and become unstuck?

AN AUTHOR'S PERSPECTIVE ON LEADERSHIP AND THE LEADER WITHIN US

The author's role as a leadership 360-degree feedback coach nourished a natural tendency to observe the leadership practices of others. Any general reflection on what causes a person to show leadership, and another not to demonstrate leadership, reduces to subtle distinctions measured in frequency of opportunity. This generates consistency for some people to demonstrate a drive to excel, or a drive to confuse.

A drive to excel becomes fueled by a vision for the future, for what could be a drive informed by listening and making decisions with minimal second guessing. Many people show a drive to see their team excel in sports, and collectively manifest that drive through purchasing team jerseys, viewing games, reading about their team, watching *Mike & Mike* to see opinions about their team, purchasing tickets to games, and even voting for taxes to support a local stadium.

This drive manifests itself in conversations about their team with others on a daily basis, even at church (just not during a sermon). People identify with this team as representative of themselves and of their city or regional area. This can occur at the high school, college, and pro sports levels.

More consistently, some of us apply a similar drive to our work. Recognizing what is important to us in our lives, we identify what we do at work and what our work organization contributes to, as contributing to something bigger than ourselves.

We typically make sacrifices for this beyond our job description, to include "how" we fulfill our role. We want the money and financial security it brings, yet some of us become players beyond a specific contract or expectation. We read all about our organization every chance we get!

What feeds people's drive more consistently through work or participation in other communities?

From where do people derive energy, determination, and that irrepressible drive to excel, to push beyond, to communicate information about their organization as if communicating about their chosen sports team?

What causes some people to delight in the face of a challenge to that which is meaningful to them? As if the actual player on the court experiencing a combination of anxiety and eagerness?

What inspires such confidence to walk the path in front of clients, in front of currently skeptical yet potential clients, to walk the path among employees or nonbelievers and do so with a sense of respectful confidence?

What makes a leader a leader? Someone who consistently connects with others?

What follows will reflect behavioral responses of many leaders across cultures and languages, across "types" as defined by psychological assessments defining and grouping people by tendencies and categorizing these in the hopes of increasing understanding among the different types. The authors propose you do not define yourselves by the types; you define yourselves by the possibilities. Think about the possibilities awaiting you as behave your way into a future waiting to be lived.

As I listen to stories of leaders and observe the leadership within us, some of the answer to what makes a leader recognized as such comes through a fundamental vision that leads this drive. Better yet, it informs this drive.

A vision that compels one to see work or time spent in a community as more than work or more than spending one's time.

A vision that gives people a sense of pursuing a calling, of making time for something with what limited time we all realize we have here on this earth in this current form.

A vision that compels creatively "what can be" overlaying "what is."

A vision that recognizes at some level that this can become a lifetime investment, not just one season to win it all.

A vision that seeks information as most new life we know seeks sunlight and moisture.

A vision that nurtures a love for achieving through ones' work, as an extension of a love for others and a love for play that forms a natural balance.

Are some people with proclaimed "titles" workaholics? Yes. However, true leadership recognizes a love for play and a love for relationship with others beyond the playing field of accomplishing lifelong pursuits.

And what is this vision? Is the vision a three-sentence mission or vision statement that people talk about loving? Can you describe a vision that excites people to love and thus to drive to excel in the face of contrary evidence?

How does this vision draw leaders and people practicing leadership, into relationship with others? One natural consequence from my observation is that leaders recognize the need to work with others, to develop a sense of team with people of similar values yet different skillsets.

When talking with visionary leaders based on assessment feedback from their workplace community, one way visionary leaders literally draw others into a sense of purpose larger than self is to draw!

A hallmark comment of "how do you promote innovative thinking and productive dialogue?" reflects encouraging others to draw out visually what they think in conversation. These "drawings" foster a tendency toward more productive conversation in relationship among groups of teams, even groups normally disparate in time and place.

Do these drawings represent one way of challenging the status quo thinking? Yes, however, promoting avenues of constructively, productively, respectfully challenging, honoring both the past and a future that some day too will become an honored past.

Think about a previous past that was once your future. What transition period led you through from a time when life was always the same to moments in life that introduced change, a new normal? Notice how these practices act in unison as if a symphony, orchestrating a sense of community focused on forward thinking?

An expression from an unknown person indicates, "There are moments that mark your life, moments when you realize nothing will ever be the same, and time is divided into two parts, before this and after this."

Replace "your life" in this statement with "your workplace community," and I believe the same occurs as a result of the influence and practice of visionary behaviors by leaders in the community.

"There are moments that mark your workplace community, moments when you realize nothing will ever be the same, and time is divided into two parts, before this and after this."

Communicating includes carefully considering the options for what meaning becomes communicated by the intention of chosen vocabulary. Powerful yet subtle distinctions of language influence the course of a conversation and the series of conversations.

"Yes, and" tends to promote a more coordinated approach in conversation among players in the conversation. A "Yes, but" tends to promote a wedge between players in the conversation.

Distinctions in language used become subtle yet powerful. Recognizing these becomes driven by one's vision for a future beyond the moment, the present issues. This "working in the subtlety of intentional language" becomes included in the business of visionary leaders when communicating.

The forward thinking prompted by visionary behaviors and a mind-set toward possibilities becomes further nourished by something less scientific and somewhat wet—establishing emotional bonds among those we encounter, whether we encounter these people on a daily basis or semi-regularly.

What behavior (actions) and language preceded by thoughts fosters an atmosphere where people want to go to work, and where respect and fairness mark descriptions of leaders in a workplace community?

In your presence, do people want to be around you, or want to be elsewhere? (Be blunt with yourself, when seeking personal growth opportunities.)

Motive through individual vanity and pride have little to no room here. I once heard how vanity and pride act much like the surface of a balloon. The larger it stretches on the outside, the larger the emptiness inside the balloon. The larger personal vanity and pride stretches the person's ego and perspective, the more shallow, the more empty on the inside. This emptiness distorts reality, creating a leader without a healthy connection with others.

What takes the place of pride and vanity?

How does humility and modesty create a reality in touch with the anxiety and desire of others around?

How does humility and modesty shift a power from one person to a power among people throughout the community?

Subtleties exist here as well that offer clues to a leader projecting from a sense of pride to a leader projecting a sense of humility. What marks a distinction between leaders who think less of the good they can accumulate and more of the good they can do (for and with others)?

One behavioral pattern of role model leadership noted that when talking with others at their desks, the leader would bend down, find a chair, kneel, or somehow find a way to position next to people seated at their desks, instead of standing over them and talk with them while they are seated. Subtle as this may sound, how might this alter any given conversation—a conversation around an issue, or a brief problem-solving conversation, or perhaps a getting-to-know-you conversation?

What further behavioral clues do role model leaders offer as insight to an internal presence rooted in humility and self-confidence? (Think how similar here, not opposite, as opposed to an internal emptiness of pride expanding a false sense of one's self in isolation.)

Hear of recruiting for the best talent as a means of competitive advantage? Once obtained, communicating regularly in such a way as to draw out that talent becomes paramount.

People of talent prefer to experience the feeling of a job well done, of contributing and being valued for their participation in creating something big, doing the work they want to do (versus need to do), and feeling respected and appreciated.

What communication describes an organization where talent is able to become, where people can "be?"

If part of one's initial response centers around asking questions, this indeed earmarks what role model communicators often cite about their workplace conversations. Asking questions that promote a sharing of alternative views, increasing capacity for new ideas leading to new platforms, new products, innovative features.

Providing clear direction, timely feedback, a desire to discuss the views of others, and expressing ideas with perspective and context when sharing information describe a workplace where one can ask, "How does one disagree without becoming disagreeable?"

Responses lead to choices when mapping the reality check of knowns with unknowns. This leads to making decisions and the reality of taking risks when incorporating methods born of new, typically unproven ideas, absent the certainty of research-based evidence.

Confident and constructive decisiveness and risk-taking are born from confident and constructive communications. (For example, "What works here?" "What do we want to have happen here?" and "What is working so far? What does this tell us?")

One pattern of leaders rated as role models for decisiveness talk about making timely decisions given the best information known at the time, being able to adapt and change given new information, and not second-guessing or looking back in regret.

Does this sound like someone such as you?

The calling card of leadership, and how it looks and sounds. "When you say this, I am thinking [that]. . . is that what you mean?"

Clear communication in the moment feeds the energy and innovative spirit of humans. This promotes the exchange of ideas born out of desire, not out of fear. Learning organization practitioner Peter Senge once stated, "It's as if we're driving down a road at night, speeding faster and faster, and at the same time we're turning our headlights down dimmer and dimmer."

A leader's conversation patterned with questions for clarity in a tone of partnership promotes the brighter headlight on the organization's or community's yet unachieved future.

Other similar questions displaying the currency of leadership? "If this was your personal family business, when choosing between alternatives (a) and (b), which one gives a better chance of becoming a money maker eight months down the road?" "In what situation might (a) be the better solution? When might decision (b) or alternative (c) be the better choice?"

Role model leaders sometimes indicate what may sound strange on the surface when describing how they behave, and how they pursue their calling in any given moment. The author finds responses like these across gender, across cultures. "I listen with what I see, first the energy, before as a means of determining what is heard."

The author believes we could conduct an intriguing seminar exploring just this statement, and role-play how that might be put into practice, to determine how what is heard becomes larger than life.

Another common question asked either within the mind of a leader, or asked of those in conversation, sounds like this: "Who else needs to know about this?" Just think to yourself as one partial self-reflection, does this question sound familiar to you? Do you hear yourself asking this question on a fairly regular basis while *living your calling of leadership? How does your leader's story read?*

When coyotes and other pack animals seek food, seek nourishment to survive, while they may not be asking this question, Do they act like as if they are asking it?

Could this become another question descriptive of one's leadership calling, feeding the survival of one's organization, a type of question nourishing one's community?

Understandably, it takes a willingness to work at it when asking this question. This speaks to communicating quickly and coherently to all parties so as not to be misunderstood downstream. Like a story, each project, each decision represents a life of its own, a story with a beginning, a tension, and a resolution of the tension in conclusion. This suggests some built-in delays, yet likely reducing rework in the future while reminding members of the organization of their personal commitment, of why they choose to be in this organization.

Do you want to be in this story? Do you want your people (employees, clients, peers, bosses, others) in this story? Do you go to church on weekends and wonder, "How can I influence a better story at work through what I hear now?"

How else does your leadership calling sound? When listening, what is your first intent to understand what the other person has to say? If you hear yourself saying "Yes, sounds plausible," think again. "The most important [initial] part of listening is not to understand what the person has to say, but to hear the person out and let them finish." How might this latter starting position change your experience when listening to others? Change the experience for others being listened to by you?

Could this relax your own nonverbal body language just a bit more to convey sincere engagement with those speaking, crying out with their voice? Could this shed some light on empathy, leading to one commenting that "I heard you say this, are you feeling [that]?"

There is a term I propose to you called "manipulative hearing." To me, manipulative hearing occurs with a more mechanical inclination to understand as quickly as possible what the other person has to say. The same speed of understanding that becomes replaced with one's own typically contrary view.

Seeking genuine listening as a feature of the currency of your leadership calling? Consider the subtle yet powerful difference—especially in situations recognizing emotions and a history at play—of changing one's starting position for listening. From one of listening to understanding what the other person has to say. To listening with the intent to hear the person (people) out and let them finish. What character traits does this call forth from within you?

It begins with being clear to oneself about one's personal intentions in the moment of any conversation.

What is the need one naturally recognizes in any given communication? Do others often think you listen showing evidence your mind is already made up? Listening to be polite?

By illustration, one story of one leader putting this to practice and how it makes money more quickly than conventional practice. The author once asked a leader rated as a role model through their assessment by others, "How do you do this, can you provide an example?" He actually cited the example set by his CEO-mentor.

As the story goes, an important meeting was to begin. Two opposing camps of employees—union and management—sitting opposite sides across from each other along an extended table. They maintained distance from each other. However, by the end of the meeting they left in cordial and collective conversation, as if one team.

This leader observed that the CEO's interaction, communication, and listening spelled the difference in change of tone. "For most of the day, the CEO asked questions and listened." He recalls the CEO reflecting, "I notice you speak with such commitment through your tone of voice. Can you tell me more about what creates such passion?"

As people on the opposite side listened to their concern or their deeper thinking, they began to see how similar they were at a fundamental level. By the day's end, it was as if a transformation had occurred.

When thinking about conversations featuring genuine questions and a desire to genuinely listen, clear communication and attentiveness to awareness of deeper issues beyond the surface provide the follow-through describing the currency of a leader's calling.

Recognizing that while matters of money are being discussed, when it is really less about money and more about pride. Sometimes giving (of respect) can occur without giving anything of substance in terms of money.

Pursuing one's leadership calling requires disagreeing without becoming disagreeable. Arguing a position instead of a point breeds inflexibility, unbending, not listening, and eventually losing. This is not in pursuit of one's calling. It becomes a pursuit of vanity and ego.

Yet be clear, giving something away and getting nothing in return can create an expectation of entitlement. Clear communication includes brief specifics as to goals to provide guidance and a target for people to work toward.

For example, which of the following provides clearer communication in your mind? "Help the client save expenses" or "Save the customer ten dollars" (and) "Save the client 20 percent of monthly or annual operating expenses." Which communication would you prefer?

Offering a degree of specificity in our everyday conversations balanced with enabling the "how" to be decided as much as possible by others supports not only attainment of goals but can become empowering.

Final thoughts on effectively communicating one's leadership calling. When an employee needs to change a behavior, the lead story to the employee is not "You did this, that is wrong." Rather "This is the behavior, and it has to change."

When stating, "Help me understand what you mean when you state. . .," this signals a request to include the context, to start from the beginning, and to be patient with the leader.

Encouraging others in the passion of one's own calling. Those sensing and pursuing their calling in leadership typically enjoy mentoring others in the same calling who are willing. When you discover a person developing other leaders, you discover a person in the pursuit of their leadership calling. Is that person you?

Stories illustrate our human condition and the role of leadership as a way to let people's light shine. Fables, fairy tales, and fiction often speak to a deeper truth. Take the story of Cinderella. Despite her mistreatment at the hands of the wicked stepmother and her sisters, no one could distinguish or destroy the beauty and grace of Cinderella. She only needed an opportunity to shine, to show who she truly was, and a prince provided her that opportunity.

Each of us is bestowed a beauty of talents and grace. As a leader, do you help potential future leaders reveal their particular light to shine through the cinders of their Cinderella phase of their career?

Through the cinders, can you see the Cinderella of energetic leadership waiting to be lived?

Through mentoring, coaching, and development, do you encourage those experiencing the fear of letting their light shine, as if a wicked stepmother shadowed them? Imagine if the character Luke Skywalker stated, "I'll let someone else do this, I can't do it?" Imagine if all of our heroes and leaders took this path of least resistance. This story was shared within a sermon on spiritually growing. It equally applies to leadership growth.

Speaking of coaching and mentoring, the authors are believers in building on the strengths of people to truly enjoy what they do and expand what they do well to do even better. Some believe in questions to encourage others to think expansively. For example, when you hear an employee indicate "I do not have the patience you have to do what you do."

One question for thought may include "When have you shown patience with others? What circumstances can you recall when you indeed acted patiently, or were appreciated for your patience?" Sometimes the proverbial light hidden under the bushel basket just needs the basket lifted so slightly for the believer to believe and act accordingly!

More on development: How does my leadership calling influence a team approach to serving our clients, our customers?

One role model leader known for developing his team's ability to serve the client more effectively established a client mind-set among his employees without sending them to "classes" and "conferences." How did he do it?

> *I inherited a team of people with no clue to the business and contracts, which were traditionally kept fairly secretive in the past. People just did their individual jobs, yet somewhat in a vacuum. This group behavior had to change. So basically, I copied the contracts, distributed them, and tested people over time. I always offered an assortment of different chocolates for right answers. Almost two years have now passed since I started this. Even I cannot believe the results, which exceeded my expectations. My people are ahead of me now when it comes to learning about and resolving customer/client issues. When problems arise, they show concern and respond. They propose ideas, solutions which result over time in revenue growth, simply because they work not for revenue growth, but for customer/client success.*

This becomes a team of "Not my job," to a team that understood basic financial implications of decisions made, understanding and talking about impacts. It becomes a team that makes it their business to understand the system implications to their own decisions.

What is more, this became a team who understood that recognized when to speak to value added in "what we do for you," during conversations—impromptu ones as well as planned ones—another way to act out "carpe diem," seize the day!

Notice how this leader acted like that prince in Cinderella, developing the team to shine their light in ways which exceeded even the leader's vision of what could be?

Development can be sending folks to a conference or experiencing a course. Development can also become a part of the daily work conversations . . . the work of changing group norms to me sounds much like the biblical reference to the dew appearing. We never quite see it form, it suddenly just appears.

A leader's journey is not always measured in timelines and milestones. Leadership includes a faith walk, a faith effort.

And there's more. . .

Developmentally focused leaders typically recognized when to gut check an employee's previous job satisfaction, by asking questions such as, "Does this (role/series of tasks) continue to turn you on, or do you find yourself becoming bored, not as excited nor feeling the adrenaline rush?" People always felt the leader's concern for them as individuals.

By prioritizing their people's needs through what they said and did, and by meeting their people's priorities, leaders in turn caused a team who will meet the leader's priorities, reflecting the organization/community priorities. This demonstrates the often-heard expression, "People won't care until they first realize you care (about them)."

Leaders who negotiated often referred to just being plain considerate as a means for achieving win-win situation in their conversation. For example, "When might be a better time . . ." and to keep the momentum going, "Unless I hear from you by [such and such time/day], you can count on me doing this and in this manner."

This beckons a call of the wild in us—natural courtesy within the context of timeframes and requirements needed by other stakeholders—always nurtured strong relationships based on trust.

Another tool to leverage when facilitating an issue of contention among people within a team, or between teams of people, was use of a strawman document. A visual describing a proposed solution seems to shift the oppositional flow from a focus between individuals and groups on opposite sides to a flow directed toward the ideas expressed in the strawman.

This shift with proper and observant facilitation can be just enough to form a replacement of the strawman with a representation of creative ideas as people work toward a solution, away from further entrenching oppositional view towards expansive and new ways of thinking and approach.

An example of proper and observant facilitation sounds like, "What if we were to look at it this way" and invites suggestions for how that could happen. Another strength of good facilitation is to allow conversations to diverge when obtaining ideas, and then recognize when to converge the conversation and create some productive outcomes.

How might this shift from diverging to converging sound from a facilitator? "What do we now know we did not know (15) minutes ago?"

An overarching lesson that more senior or seasoned leaders learn when it comes to development is recognizing the need for being available and accessible to people when an employee's personal needs causes this preemptive question to be heard by the leader: "Do you have a minute?" Two factors must be understood by the leader, one long term, one immediate.

Over the long term, the seasoned leader understands how to let go of the insatiable desire to accomplish tasks—a desire that feeds an immediate gratification over and over again. Some leaders become selected as leaders partly because of their predisposition to finish things and get the job done.

Over time, leaders understand that an expansion of accomplishing tasks includes knowing when to stop what one is doing, and truly be present when hearing an employee say, "Do you have a minute?" Not answering the phone or responding to text messages—attention to electronic devices—ceases during the ensuing conversation. Believe me, little things become noticed!

Oh yes, and the more immediate factor leaders must recognize when hearing "Do you have a minute?" It will take longer than a minute. Meaning, do not attempt to rush through, and be relatively relaxed. Do this, and you are the leader who promotes future Cinderella experiences.

When in a high-pressure, fast-paced environment (for the 99 percent of our readers):

Let's face it, some of us thrive on our personal drive, and enjoy high stress! As one leader described himself based on role model markings recognizing his drive to excel, he replied, "A person cannot achieve all he possibly can, unless he takes on more than he can possibly achieve."

Others of us handle those fast-paced periods of time, although we prefer an office hammock when given a choice. Regardless of these extremes and in-between, what follows shows a pattern of what role model leaders think and what they say and do to promote productive results even under times of high duress.

And let's put one thing on the table for some of our readers. Do you find yourself able to identify any pattern of crisis mode because you yourself are a procrastinator? There, it has been stated. One disclaimer here is this: If you are, the following suggestions are not intended to enable a dysfunction of delaying in such a way as to create opportunities for crisis and tension! Now that this is on the table. . .

When quickly assessing risk in the decision process, leaders often cite asking questions such as "What is the short-term impact? What are the long-term impacts?" "Can we live with these short-term, long-term consequences?" and "If I/we decide NOT to do this, here is the positive, negative and neutral impacts." In other words, leaders discuss pros and cons fairly quickly with those who share a stake in the matter.

Another perspective some leaders note around resolving problems with urgency is there is no time for assessing blame, pointing the finger, finding out who dun'it; rather, instead of asking "What is right? What is wrong?" leaders change their language in these occasions of urgency to "What is working? What is not working?"

This subtle shift in language is like the subtle one degree difference between freezing rain and its experience, and just plain rain. Both are slippery, but the freezing rain can mean failure. Plain cold rain may mean discomfort on the way to resolution.

Another message from role model decision makers? They tend to not second guess themselves later. Rather, they understand making the decision with the best information available at the time. And what's more? If they do not know what they do not know at the time of deciding, even if that adversely impacts consequences, they continue thinking about how to adjust moving forward.

It becomes a pattern of think, decide, act, adjust, think, decide, act, adjust. This is not a living for the perfectionistic at heart (returning us full circle to the disclaimer toward those who procrastinate).

A message for the perfectionists among us from leaders? The difference in language comes down to this: when assessing risk and seeking solutions/ actions to take, it becomes less about looking for the "best" solution. It becomes all about seeking the "best acceptable" solution. What does this mean to me? What does this suggest to me?

Combining decisiveness with a brief revisit of career development, one leader who assessed a role model for showing confidence and composure amid unpleasant or frustrating situations offered the following. "When I decide whether to shy away from an opportunity, I generally assess two possible motives. First, am I wanting to shy away from the opportunity because I feel guilty? Then probably too much going on. However, if I am wanting to shy away because I feel afraid or uncomfortable? Likely this becomes the opportunity I should take."

Can this guidance apply to me? Can this guidance productively help people I coach and mentor when facing a career opportunity/move?

Integrity walks hand-in-hand with risk-taking and decisiveness. How often the author hears leaders say "I will readily own up to my mistakes."

So too does a positive versus a negative mind-set. A story I once heard featured the positive farmer and the negative farmer. When rain fell, the positive farmer said, "Thank you for watering our crops." The negative farmer said, "Yes, but if this keeps up, it will rot the roots away." Sun came out, and the positive farmer states, "Thank you for the sunshine nourishing our crops. We are going to have a bountiful harvest." The negative farmer said, "Yeah, but this keeps up, it'll burn out the roots, and we'll have no crop."

One day, the two farmers went bird hunting, and the positive farmer brought along his new bird dog he wanted to show off; he was so proud of it. They waited in a small boat. Before long, a bird flew over and "boom" the positive farmer brought it down in the lake. He told his buddy, "Watch what this dog can do!" Can you believe, that dog leapt out of the boat, running on top of the water, and returned with the bird, while still running on top of the water? The dog placed the bird right at the positive farmer's feet in the boat. Beaming with pride from ear to ear, the positive farmer said, "What do you think of that?" To which the farmer, in a disgusted tone, replied, "Just what I thought. That dog can't even swim."

Positive role model thinking is always vigilant for preventing that negative thinking from putting a drag on the group's performance and results.

To establish context for the next story, the author introduces this true personal tale. It happened while attending a professional development session with hundreds of K–12 teachers participating. The speaker opened by asking, "In order to know my audience, a show of hands please, how many of you are elementary school teachers?" Following a show of hands, he asked, "How many of you, through a show of hands, are high school teachers?" He concluded by asking and stating, "Will the middle school teachers please stand up??" [After a brief pause] "May we now have a moment of silence."

This next story could leave you not only silent, but speechless.

This story comes from a colleague of the authors, Dr. Darylann Whitemarsh, from her days teaching in the middle school. I think of the current and former substitute teachers among us, as well as an example of what Stephen Covey once stated, communicating people's worth and potential so clearly that they are inspired to see it in themselves. Now the story:

When I was teaching, I too felt the need to have detailed lesson plans when a sub went into my classroom. I remember when I had to go to a state educator's meeting, I left extremely detailed plans for my sub. But unfortunately the sub never showed up because the school administrators overlooked hiring one.

My students didn't know that, so when no sub showed up for first hour, the class leader for the week took over. She picked up the lesson and followed it. The students handed in all their homework and when the bell rang they left for the next class.

Then the second hour middle school students entered my classroom. The problem here was it was normally my "prep" hour, but I was helping the "teacher who taught behavior disabilities," so my detailed lesson plans for that hour went again to the student leader. He got all 12 kids under control and taught the class. They followed the lesson plan and turned in their assignments. Now this could have been a real problem because these kids were "extreme" behavior problems. But they were learning to be people of character, so they just applied the principles that day in my class.

Then third hour came along and the student leader for that hour said "Something is wrong" and marched down to the principal's office. The principal then called in someone to take over. You see when you are teaching students about character, you give them the opportunity to model it.

That is why I always had student leaders for the week. They would do minor leadership activities in the class such as, take attendance to the office, collect assignments and put them in the in-box, etc. They all sure did an excellent job in the class that day.

For lunch the next day I bought "each" student a personal pizza. They were thrilled! And, we talked about what wonderful examples of people of character that they displayed that day. That gave the teachers in the lounge something to talk about and to see that teaching character to kids works!

What does this story reveal to you about diversity of integrity, diversity of leadership, from a very young age? How different are the responses of three different students, all practicing leadership? Suppose this happened in your school and this is our lunchroom.

Suppose this happened among three junior leaders in your workplace and this is our lunch room. What would you want to share with your colleagues?

Could this promote a shift in awareness among some teachers/leaders as to the potential capacity for leadership among their students/employees?

What messages do you hear in the midst of high-stress events that either promote or inhibit such spontaneous acts of leadership, of ownership, in the moment when most needed?

What if you shared this story in your community?

What questions could promote a conversation about how things are really going—the theory in use, so to speak?

WHAT DID I HEAR AT THE TOP OF THE STAIRS?

As a kid growing up, this author's family lived in a two-story colonial. On a rare night your author quietly proceeded to the top of the steps. Why? There was a need to hear what "they" might be saying about me! Other times out of concern and curiosity about how they were doing if an issue or a problem seemed to exist.

What do we as leaders hear at the top of our steps, on the upper floor, when listening to our employees' chatter or to our students' talk about what mattered? What do angels hear from the gates of heaven's top step?

What heaven's calling have you inherited from God, as you journey in grace? To what are you called to do, to be? How does that reflect what one hears at the top of the steps, on the upper floor?

A pastor once stated, "Who wouldn't leave 99 sheep to save one measly sheep? No one, but God." We have good company on our journey, even though sometimes God feels distant.

How does one experience God's mercy, and how can one be merciful? Do you allow God to be merciful to you? Or do you feel not worthy? If you allow

God to be merciful to you, can you become more able to turn show mercy toward another?

Jesus boiled it down to one thing, "Love one another." Yet there was a qualifier . . . "as I have loved you." How do we take what we listen to through our time with our spiritual community, and let that guide our leadership thinking, behaving, and mind-set?

Jesus said, "Blessed are the poor in heart." While I do not believe excluding lottery winners, notice we do not hear "Blessed are those who won the lottery." Counting our blessings to the author does not suggest adding them up and listing them. It means paying attention to our blessings.

In doing so, we recognize the sacredness and presence of our God, even during times when we may feel abandoned or removed from His presence. "I for one appreciate you biting your tongue in there for the last hour, and I know practicing patience is tough. . ."

As the giver determines the meaning of the gift, the leader determines the meaning of his or her leadership.

Availability—the best ability is availability. [Accessible and available]

The intent of this book is to help you be ready, a process mind-set, as opposed to getting ready for leading, an event driven. The wish, indeed the prayer, becomes our orientation toward "being ready," an important distinction to a deeper appreciation and thus a deeper practice of our leadership, our connecting with other human beings.

We often hear "What would you do if you were told you would die in the near future, even this very day?" To think of calling certain people, to think of doing . . . reflects "Getting ready," appears event driven. Could a sense of unusual calm prevail if all along we were living, being ready?

What if you were told "Tonight you no longer lead." What mind-set would you experience if you felt a need to "get ready" compared to the mind-set of "being ready?"

Would the need to part with some heartfelt words to those you lead be as important to do when always having been in the process of "being ready?" Do I say "I am ready," or do I respond "I will get ready?" The subtle distinction between preparing to be (think traps of procrastination) and being who I am lies in the balance.

What significance or recognition or insight will you reaffirm or gain through your time absorbing what becomes key for you in these pages?

How will this steady you in a life's temporary journey often beset by the turbulence of connecting with people of different perspectives, viewpoints, and beliefs?

As you meet your maker, what story about your life would you wish to share? More specifically, what story about your leadership would you be able to share?

To what piece of your legacy would you refer?

Remember, who is in control? God is. What a relief it's not me! Something one learns from listening at the top of the steps.

NOTE

1. Wait for the second marshmallow. (2012, February 2). *The Voice Tribune*. Retrieved from https://voice-tribune.com/columns/don-mcnay/wait-for-the-second-marshmellow/.

Chapter 2

Reflections of Mike Singletary on Leadership Experience

Reflecting previously on the vision, one's calling as a leader, and the emphasis on development of others, note how what has been discussed weaves through responses of a Hall of Fame football player and coach, Mike Singletary. Does one see the self-reflection and continual growth in one's own journey reflected through Mike's self-reflection and personal growth?

We thank Mike for sharing his reality through this interview with grace, humility, and tough honesty.

1. *What is a moment in your leadership experience you would relive if you could and why?*

Mike: If I could relive one leadership experience, it would be half time of the San Diego Chargers game, my second year as head coach with the 49ers. I could have handled the half-time in such a better way. There were side effects which I allowed to influence my thinking. We had two All-Pro Linebackers, who banged up really should not have been playing. They could only play with one hand. We had one of our best defensive players outside of those two guys, thrown out of the game! We went into half-time down I think 17–0, and I really wanted the quarterback to put the team on his back and for the offense to pick it up and prove to the country that the 49ers were a good football team. Very pivotal game for us, we had failed to score on fourth and 1 from the end zone. So we went into half-time and I was really angry with our quarterback and our offense.

I let it all hang out and said things like, "Do you want the guys on defense to play on offense as well? Do you want them to play on both sides of the ball?" So yelling at them, I did not use wisdom, and my comments in terms of how badly we were playing, I would love to take that back. To take a moment that was to be a very pivotal moment, and instead of pouring gasoline on the fire,

51

be able [instead] to divert some of that negative energy into positive energy. It was a great time that if I had to do over again, I would just stop. Go into half time, get the quarterback in front of the team, and instead of delivering that message, that was negative, I would change it, and tell him that we have the game exactly where we want it. We are on national television, and as a game we had to win in order to go to the playoffs, I would have told him, "This is your finest moment and you have the chance to define for the country who you are as quarterback. Go out in the second half, take the team, put us on your back, and take us to victory."

I believe it would have changed that game, I believe it would have changed the season. That comes first to mind [in response to your question].

Marty: There is a phrase from Jack Canfield, sharing an equation E + R = O. Events plus our Response equals the Outcome. We cannot control or even predict events in our life as they occur. What the equation suggests is that what we can control or influence is our response to those events, to influence the Outcome. Thank you for also describing that equation through your real-life reflection.

A follow-up question, How have you leveraged that personal lesson as a leader moving forward, to where it became a different message that you communicated in another situation that may have been the reason for this experience to begin with?

Mike: The greatest opportunity I have had as a coach, why I am coaching today, when I got fired that year and left San Francisco and went to Minnesota for three years, then left Minnesota—the thing I have most learned as a leader, [is that] too many of our leaders today are really watered down. Our country today is not leading. As much as we try to preach tolerance, our country today does not tolerate leadership. What we have today in our country is more managers than leaders. [One only need] question just look at the number of committees that we have, instead of leaders making decisions.

Marty: At the time a Senior VP of Walt Disney, referring to leadership, cited common phrases which suggest killing leadership, killing creativity, and representing management. One of those phrases is, "Let's form a committee to work on this." I served as an *Odyssey of the Mind* coach and was able to attend the first ever world conference in Washington DC in 1996, featuring speaker Val Oberle, who at the time was a senior VP for Disney. She directly spoke to your previous observation through a level of how we speak.

You took me right back to that.

2. *Thinking of prior adverse situations, what keeps your resolve despite evidence to the contrary? Events in life that suggest to us to quit and do*

something else. What keeps you focused? What keeps you resolved, helps you persist in spite of contrary evidence?

Mike: The first thing that comes to mind is Theodore Roosevelt's comment in a speech about the critic . . . that it is not the critic who deserves the praise, but the one in the ring whose face is marred with sweat and blood. It is not the critic who points out how he erred, but the one who gets back up and tries again [who deserves the praise]. The critic will never know either defeat or victory. He will only be able to talk about what he sees someone else doing.

So for me, the number one reason I have not gone on and done something else, is that I believe this in one of my callings in my life. I believe that this is a journey that will affect my destiny. A journey that will affect my destiny. Trust me, I have wanted to do something else. But I believe if I were to do something else, I would miss my destiny. I love what I do, I love to be a coach, I am glad that God called me into coaching.

Yet I also realize, when I became a head coach in the league for the first time, I had been in the league for five years, now competing against coaches who had been coaching 20 or 30 years. What I saw around the league in terms of leadership was what guys had learned from other guys. That is why I got out after my third year at Minnesota because I looked around and saw everyone copying everyone else. This is the way you gracefully lose a game so that ownership does not look at you and fire you.

This is the way you control your team in the locker room so that your players won't quit on you. It was a how to . . . but I did not see anyone really standing out. I saw coaches enraged on Sundays and praying on Mondays that they did not get fired.

So I think leadership, as I have known and studied leaders, you know it when it is in the room, you know when it is present. And today, it is not present very often, and when it is, in today's time it is not embraced, it is ostracized. People do not understand it nor recognize that leadership is what has made America great.

When you live in an age of mediocrity, leadership seems harsh. Leadership seems like something absurd, because you just don't see it any more. It becomes evident when you see what is happening at the lowest levels of our country, when you give everyone on the team a trophy, when they did not earn it. A team that runs up a score is going to be called bullies.

I get concerned sometimes for our country, because leadership is what made America great. In order for us to keep America great, leadership will have to lead the way.

Marty: Personally for me, I often thought about the media today as almost being too much about themselves, trying to create the news as opposed to reporting on the news. You helped me think about this in a different way when you referred to a quote by Theodore Roosevelt. So I too am growing listening to you.

3. Who mentored you on leadership, and how did they most impact you? Do you have a particular person who comes to mind who mentored you? What was it they in particular shared, communicated, or modeled for you?

Mike: Fortunately I have a few.

The first mentor I had was my high school coach, Coach Oliver Brown. Oliver Brown came from nothing, and fought his way to become an educator and coach. He was consistent every day. He really cared for his players and was so passionate about the development of young men. In that poor area I lived in, in an African American community, everyone respected Coach Brown. I don't care if you were a drug dealer of if you were a prostitute, when you came across Coach Brown, you either went the other way, or you said, "Hi Coach Brown. How you doing Coach Brown?" When he saw someone who needed help, he was very compassionate, very empathetic. He was on you when he knew that you needed it, but he loved you when you needed it as well.

The mentor I saw in college (there were several of them), Coach Corky Nelson was my defensive coach. A strong word to use, but at the time I hated him. He worked me so hard every day, from the day I got there until the day I left. I really did not understand why he picked on me. He picked on me every day it seemed like. It was fifteen years later when I had my own son. I was coaching my son. My oldest son had a hard head and was stubborn like I was. One day coaching him, he was looking out of the window, frustrated, with tears in his eyes, and it brought back memories of Nelson in college, and how he never gave up on me. I am saying "You have no idea how hard I am trying to make you see how you can make you the best that you can be. I don't have to say anything to you. I don't have to push you. I could give up on you and find somebody else." And when I thought about that, I had to pull over and call my college coach Nelson who I had not talked to since I had left. I told him how I appreciated him, and what he did for me. And we became friends.

[Recall how Bobbie Bowden referred to himself as a father figure to his players, and the tie-in with Mike here calling his former coach when discovering something his own son taught him in their growing relationship?]

[For our readers, have you previously "hated" and yet, with further experience, revisited the relationship with a different perspective expressing gratitude? Have you transformed what was distance and absence into closeness and connection?]

Marty: Is he still alive to this day Mike?

Mike: No, he passed a few years ago.

Coach Teaff was my college head coach, and another mentor. He was very consistent. Everything he did showed consistency. He was a gentleman, he was a Christian man who loved God and was devoted to his family. He took it upon himself to really develop me. I watched him. I rode around with him when he would invite me to go with him when he was asked to speak at times. He placed a lot of trust in me. Things like, if he caught a guy doing something wrong, he would say, "Mike, I promised this kid's mother he would get a degree, but this is his third time doing drugs. I had told him if I caught him again he was going home."

He would ask me in tears, what I think he should do. He would say that kid has nowhere to go. He does not have anything to go back to.

Then I said, "Coach, I have one question for you. What did you tell him?" Coach says "I told him I would send him home if I caught him again." I said, "Then that is what you have to do."

He trusted me enough to lean on me and help me develop the leadership role I had, and constantly allowed me to develop as a leader.

Coach Buddy Ryan was another mentor who taught me how to think in football. Taught me how to kook at players and see talent.

The greatest lesson I learned from Buddy was his ability to listen to someone like me when I asked him to drop a lot of the stuff we were doing. Even though he was very bright, we were ineffective, because our guys could not think as fast as the responsibilities that we had. When we began to cut down on our responsibilities, we played faster, and our defense just took off.

That was because Buddy listened to me, after I went around and asked the guys "What is it that you need in order to be a better player?" We need more walkthroughs and we need to cut down on the stuff that we are doing. Buddy cursed me out, closed the door, but he did it. Next day we were doing more walkthroughs. And we cut back significantly on the things that we were running.

Our defense became something different.

Marty: A couple things in my mind Mike. One, less is more. You recognized it, your players recognized it, and Buddy Ryan recognized it. Secondly back to Coach Teaff. What you reminded me through Coach Teaff's leadership and mentoring of you is that sometimes when we let our vulnerability show, that is when we become most strong. Coach Teaff was most strong with you when he was showing vulnerability with you. In his time of need, revealing his need. And you then practiced leadership in response, to your mentor. So thank you. Really profound for me to hear this.

4. *If you had a question on leadership you wish someone would ask, what might that be?*

Mike: I would say a question, every leader needs to clarify what their non-negotiables are. Important for me, and I believe speaks to the kind of leader you are. If I know your non-negotiables, I pretty much know whether you are going to be successful or not.

Marty: Those deeper questions may reveal to us the non-negotiables.

Before my surprise question, did you feel like your focus ever changed from being a leader on the playing field to being a leader as a coach? Thinking of team leaders, vice presidents, executive, etc. and coach, owner for you, what changed for you regarding leadership from when you were a Chicago Bear, on that playing field, and Baylor University, to when you became coach?

Mike: First of all when you are a player, a coach on the field. I used to look at *Braveheart* and other movies—the general sends their soldiers, sits back and watches them fight, now send this guy, now that one. As a leader, you need to be out there leading the charge. Well, as a player, you are on the ground crew, you are the foot soldier, you are leading the attack.

Because I am in the battle, I can get emotional. I can get frustrated, I can get mad, I can even hit a guy, "Come on man let's get going." And be even more respected for it because I am with them, I am in it with them, I am amongst them. That is one style of leadership, on the ground as with those foot soldiers. On the ground, in that locker room with them, you are bleeding and sweating and hurting with them . . . with them, hurting with them.

As a coach, when I took a step back, I had to think about that and ask, "Well, why do you ask me to coach? You know my temperament. You know who I am. You have seen me, you created me. Why do you call me 'coach' when I have to change?"

It was interesting to me that I had to take a step back and recreate myself. Not recreate my energy, my passion, my intensity—don't touch that. But it is how it is channeled. Because I am on the sideline and I am not a foot solider. Now even if I am pointing the finger. So now, rather than getting on the players from a distance . . . I am not out there hoofing it with them, I am not out there getting embarrassed with them, or at least they cannot see it. I am not getting hurt, not bleeding. I am calling calls.

What I have to do now is those coaches that are with me on that sideline, those are the guys that [are] how I was to act on the field, now, when we are away from the players, challenging those coaches. Having them understand their responsibility, and understanding what we have to do and the preparation and the execution that must be administered to the players. At the highest level of excellence, and anything less than that is unacceptable.

So I learned that it is not the players as a coach when I am on the sideline [as] I need to address those who are with me on the sideline. Because now I am pointing at those players, I am not out there with them. I have to make sure those guys on the sidelines are with those players. And make sure they understand the excellence that is expected of them that they are administering to the players all through the week.

So when we are on the sidelines, it is not the players that I am holding responsible, it is the coaches that I am depending on, to deliver my message.

Make sense?

Marty: Yes!

5. *(Time permitting, first about your nicknames, then about the on-field prayer circles)*

Marty: About 20 minutes before calling you, I Googled you. I discovered you have been called by two nicknames—Samurai Mike, and Minster of Defense, because you were an ordained minister.

Mike: I use that [term ordained minister] carefully. I have married people and [served] funerals, but I am very careful to say that I am not an ordained minister—someone who is called to preach. If you see me, there are three things that are really important to me. It is the Bible, my family, and football. So people say, you gotta be a pastor, but I am not. But those two nicknames are correct.

Marty: I was just curious, if you were ever part of those prayer circles, immediately following the end of a football game, in the middle of the field with players from both sides if they desire, how would you describe those circles, as being a part of those circles? Is it like bringing you back more quickly to life itself, because of how you all are when you kneel like that? What is that experience like?

Mike: As you go out and compete against one another, I think the prayer at the end of the game expresses the good will of why you are playing the game. I feel I play the game to glorify the Lord. I want to do everything that I did and give everything that I had to give thanks to God that I can do this and that I came out on the other side and I am not hurt.

And so to me, this gives an opportunity to say, "Hey, are you ok? I am ok. Let's pray and thank God for getting through another game and until we see each other again."

Marty: A great way to wrap this, I thank you Mike.

Mike: Thank you, sir.

Chapter 3

Expanding the Leader's Perspectives

PERSPECTIVE 1: WHAT IS YOUR RECORDER PLAYING?

There is a bible verse, Proverbs 23:7, which states, "For as he thinketh in his heart, so is he." What a powerful statement! How we think predisposes our action and directly reflects what we do and what we become. This means that we aren't victim of circumstances. Instead, we have the ability to influence our success. In fact Steve Beecham, entrepreneur and author of *Bass Ack-wards* and *What's Your Buzz*, believes that our self-talk is responsible for as much as 99 percent of success.

Our self-talk or inner recording can affect our effectiveness as a leader. Too often our self-talk may be negative. What happens after you've done something embarrassing? Does your inner voice say, "Well that was dumb"? What if you haven't even done anything wrong, but your self-talk is just as critical? "Don't speak up now and show your smallness."

This *destructive* type of self-talk causes you to question yourself so that you can soon become paralyzed with doubt and uncertainty. Ultimately, you are your only competition. It is not a competitor or the other business; it is only you competing with yourself to be the best you can be.

Self-talk should be beneficial. It should be encouraging you to do your best, to be your best. For some people, self-talk is about identifying your purpose. What is it that you offer that no one else does? What talents or abilities do you bring to the table?

When you realize you do have assets to bring to your leadership role, then you need to encourage yourself often! Self-talk or the recorder shouldn't just be playing occasionally. It should be in constant loop mode, where you are continually telling yourself that you are the woman, you are the man, serving the enterprise!

Some people can even be driven by their past, such as having to out-work everyone to be successful or feel like they have to prove something from their past. These people have learned to play a recording that encourages them to work harder and to never quit. The following stories illustrate these concepts.

Story

Steve shared during our interview about his friend Tony Phillips. They went to high school together and Tony was a good athlete even though he was smaller than everyone else. He played all sports and had offers to play at the collegiate level. He worked hard, experienced some breaks, and ultimately wound up being drafted by the Oakland A's. He played several years for the Oakland A's and then was traded and played for a few different teams over approximately a seventeen-year career, including two world series appearances and one world series championship.

Steve said they met about twenty years later when a friend's daughter was getting married in Atlanta. Because Tony had flown into town, Steve offered to shuttle him around all weekend since they were attending the same wedding functions like golfing, rehearsal dinner, etc.

During the time together, Steve noticed that Tony constantly used the phrase "My stuff always works out" when he was talking about how he had been successful. Steve asked him how long he had been using that phrase and Tony replied, "I have been saying it since I was six years old." He said, "Steve, I was smaller than everyone else, and I had to work harder than everyone else. I remember during one of my rec games that someone, maybe my mom, made the statement that I always make things work out when I'm playing, and it stuck with me." Tony said he may say it hundreds of times a week because it is how he keeps himself pushing forward.

Tony shared with Steve that not everything was easy, and that he did have setbacks, but that deep down he knew he could do what it takes to ultimately be successful because he had developed the mind-set throughout the years that "My stuff always works out!"

Steve shared another story of attending a banquet in Atlanta where he happened to be seated next to boxing champion Evander Holyfield. Steve said during the breakfast, he leaned over and asked Evander, "What tape do you play in your head?" At first, Evander asked him, "What?" But after he explained, Evander said that he did indeed have a recording that he played over and over.

Evander said when he was younger that he was small and that he was bullied a lot. So his mom took him to a gym to learn how to box and defend himself. Around the age of thirteen, he was preparing for a match that everyone thought he would win. He lost the match and when he got home he told his mom that he was going to quit boxing. He said, "My mother grabbed me by my collar, and said, son I didn't raise you to be quitter!"

Evander was seventeen and already considered to be one of the best boxers in the country. He had a match which would allow him to make Olympic team. Favored in the match, again he lost. So, he went home depressed and once again told his mom that he was quitting boxing for good.

However, this time his uncle was sitting in the room and said, "Oh you're going to be a quitter like your daddy?" Evander said, "I didn't know my dad, but I knew I wasn't going to be a quitter like him. Now, no matter what I'm going through, I never give up, because my mom didn't raise a quitter."

Finally, Steve shared his own story about what he is playing on his recorder. He said, "I didn't have a background where I felt I had to prove himself or struggling with issues from my past. But what I realized is that I have a purpose. There is something the world needs that only I have to offer. And if I am not going to do it, then who will? So I feel like I have a purpose, that I have talents to share that the world needs. So my recording tells me that I need to helping others. When I am helping others improve their lives then I can't fail."

Takeaway

What is the script of your inner self-talk predominantly familiar to you? Is it productive, reminding you of your purpose, of who you are?

If not, what is a script that could begin to replace the unproductive one?

What is a script that you could adopt, that promotes your best assets, and that sheds light on your purpose for being? (Hint: Something that serves others usually returns tenfold.)

PERSPECTIVE 2: ENCOURAGE EFFORT BUT REWARD RESULTS

In our culture, it seems that we have conditioned students, and even adults, to believe they should be rewarded for any effort they put forth. Whether it is a student who thinks he or she should get credit for simply turning in an assignment or the typical example of every player getting a trophy simply for participating.

However, rewarding effort is a dangerous habit because it can make people complacent and accept mediocrity as the norm. Part of the problem is that we don't place people in positions to use their strengths and be successful, so we think we need to motivate them by rewarding their effort, even if they can't produce the results needed.

Rewarding weaknesses is basically the same as bribery.

However, when we utilize the strengths of people in the roles, then the potential to be successful is raised exponentially, so there is less need to focus on effort, and the potential for desired results is almost certain. For example, think about someone who enjoys working out and thus doesn't need to be rewarded for going to the gym. Their desire to improve their health is the only motivation they really need.

Story

Andy Rockwood, a business consultant, shared his interaction with a business a few years ago on this topic.

Andy was talking with a business owner who was angry because one of his sales people spent most afternoons on the golf course. "I'd like to play golf too," he fumed, "but no-o-o-o, I'm stuck here in the office trying to keep this business going!" He asked if the salesman was on his numbers. "Yeah, in fact he's way over them, but that's not the point! His behavior sets a bad example for everyone else."

"So he sets a bad example for the other sales people who aren't making their numbers?" Andy asked. The owner said nothing. "It seems to me," he said, "he sets a very good example for his colleagues. He's showing them what can happen when you produce results."

Another example comes from health coach Stephanie Scocchera. She shared that she doesn't use rewards as a method of motivation. Because then the focus becomes on the reward rather than the end result. How she works around this is to focus on strengths of her clients. For example, if someone needs to lose weight, then she focuses on his or her strengths to help the person lose weight.

For example, if they benefit more from doing high reps with weights versus doing cardio, then that is what she will prescribe. Stephanie believes, "Some of us (myself included) are fortunate enough that we don't NEED rewards as the experience is enough. I have been this way ever since I was little and I believe this is where it began for those of us who are intrinsically motivated. While I don't NEED a reward, I like rewards and still reward myself from time to time. So the key is to make goals that are shorter where results can be rewarded more consistently, rather than having one long term goal, for example."

The key is to find activities they are most successful at doing so she will only need to encourage them and not constantly reward them. When they get to their goal, then the reward is even that much sweeter.

As Stephanie explained, "I believe there is a way to transform behaviors and make it so rewards are not necessary. It takes a combination of motivation AND inspiration. Reading, listening, and being still are wonderful ways to be inspired."

This is why it is important to focus on employees as individuals with different strengths and abilities, rather than trying to implement a one-size-fits-all method, which usually requires a lot of rewarding of effort to get anything accomplished.

Takeaway

The point is that it makes no sense to begrudge our high performers just because they make it look easy. It would make more sense to hold them up as role models for everyone else. Likewise, it makes no sense to reward our underachievers just because they're working at it so darn hard.

While it pains our sensibilities, if someone tries really hard but can't produce the results we expect, then we either need to adapt his or her role to his or her strengths, or we may need to let that person go someplace where his or her hard work can lead to success.

PERSPECTIVE 3: EFFECTIVE LEADERS MAKE MISTAKES BUT NOT EXCUSES

Have you ever made a mistake? The more appropriate question may be, how many mistakes have you made today? Oftentimes, leaders do not like to make mistakes and when they do there may be a tendency to want to make excuses for the mistake. However, as the key point suggests, with mistakes, you can make them worse by making excuses.

Sam Silverstein, author of *No More Excuses*, shares that leaders have to be accountable. Many people see accountability as being upward focused, meaning that you are accountable only to those who are over you. But, as he points out, effective leaders know that they are just as accountable, if not more so, to the people that they lead.

When we do own up to our mistakes, there may be the tendency to gloss over it as no big deal. We may say, yes we made a mistake, so let's just move on. But glossing over a mistake without taking ownership and reflecting upon it may lead to the mistake being made again, or consequences to the mistake lingering. But, it becomes just as important not to dwell on the mistake to the extent that it affects you or new decisions negatively.

Effective leaders will learn how to balance the effect of a mistake. For example, getting a speeding ticket is bad, but not as bad as getting a DUI, and so the consequences and response to them are different. So a leader learns to take responsibility for his or her mistakes but also understands how to appropriately address the consequences of the mistake as well.

Story

A great example we see with this concept is with head coaches. Coach Bobby Bowden, who happens to be the winningest coach in Division 1 football history, shared his own experiences during an interview with me a couple of years ago. Like other great coaches, he said that when it comes to winning he would credit his players for how hard they played and his coaches for their preparation.

However when they lost, he would always accept the responsibility for not properly preparing the players. He would admit he made mistakes, but he would not make excuses for it. The point he made was one of the effective leaders. He gave his coaches a lot of latitude in preparation and let them use their strengths because that's what he hired them to do, but at the end of the day, he was the one who sat in the head coaches chair, and he was the one who was ultimately responsible for what happened.

The author's friend, Bill Chalmers, shared a great illustration of the effects of mistakes. He said that when it comes to mistakes he uses the example of a five-gallon bucket of water. Bill shared, "Imagine having a five-gallon bucket of the freshest water from an artic glacier. If I were to offer you a drink, you would probably drink it without hesitation and it would be the best drink of water you ever tasted. But, now imagine if I were to drop a turd in the bucket of water, would you take a drink? Of course not! But what if I scooped it out and it was no longer in the water, now would you take a drink? More than likely not."

Bill continued, "Even though I removed 'the mistake' its effect is still lingering and you would not want to drink the water. Much like mistakes in business, even when you make a mistake, you may need to do more than simply correct the mistake."

Think about a bad experience with a company or organization; even if they correct the problem, it still leaves a bad taste in your mouth as well.

Takeaway

Considering other stories in here, it serves the reflecting on a mistake by considering lessons learned. Be mindful, and be vigilant for the remaining good, for leveraging what positives come from the mistake.

In the spirit of generative and genuine learning moving forward, let the mistake live comfortably to further inform others in the time of their need.

Turn that future day's mistake into sharing lessons learned in natural conversation, such as "One thing I previously learned you may now want to consider is when I did . . . I learned from that. . . . "

What other takeaways productively come to mind for you?

PERSPECTIVE 4: IF YOU HAVE NEVER FAILED, HAVE YOU TRIED HARD ENOUGH?

Failure has become a four-letter word in our culture. In schools, we have, in many ways, watered down the depth of a curriculum so students can meet a minimum standard on a test. You may not learn a lot, but at least you won't fail.

In the political arena, there is much talk about the millennial generation, who can't handle failure, or opposition of any kind. While this may be a generalization, there does seem to be less resilience and what we call stick-to-it-iveness in our younger generation. Sadly, this mentality means that people are scared to take risks or think outside the box in fear of repercussions from their "failures."

Part of the issue with failure is that we place so much emphasis on our weaknesses rather than our talents. As discussed in other sections, whether it is a student in the classroom, or an employee performance review, the tendency is to focus on weaknesses, what is not working, or areas of growth.

When this creates the anticipated focus, then we are either afraid or lack motivation to be resilient or to face the potential of failure. However, a focus on our strengths and the strengths of those we lead generates an antidote to failure. Failure becomes less daunting or final in form.

Ironically, even the most basic skills, such as walking, have actually been fine-tuned through failure. As a toddler, did you stand up and walk perfectly on your first attempt? Of course not. You stumbled like a drunk person, fell on your face, and stood back up (maybe even climbed back up) to repeat the process again.

Think of when you tried something new, such as snow skiing. Were you an expert on the first try? No, but if you are now a good skier, it is because you pushed yourself to try harder, even when you were falling more than you were actually skiing. Even an Olympic skier, like Lindsey Vonn, was not able to ski the first time she tried, but much like walking, she learned to become a world-class skier. When she leaned to ski, she didn't remain on the bunny slope either. She remained resilient as each level became more difficult and didn't let failure keep her from becoming world class.

There is an old adage that even an expert was once a novice. The only way to ultimately succeed is to push yourself beyond your comfort zone, be willing to take chances, and yes even fail. In fact, expect it.

How many people literally failed to live up to their fullest potential because they were afraid to fail? And how many people have failed to live up to their fullest potential because they weren't resilient in their failure to reflect and grow from it?

Excellence isn't taught, but rather it is developed through resilience and improving when you fail.

Story

While some people see failure as being fatal or the end of a dream, others see failure as part of the road to success. A now well-known man was once fired from a newspaper because the editor said he lacked creativity. This man failed on multiple occasions as an actor, entrepreneur, and even as an animator. This man, Walt Disney, had many failures before he created one of the most recognized names and brands in the world.

When asked about his success, Walt Disney focused on the fact that he had to overcome many obstacles, setbacks, and failures before he finally succeeded!

Walt was once quoted as saying, "Get a good idea, and stay with it. Dog it, and work at it until it's done, and done right." In picking himself up and in learning from his mistakes and moved on. He said: "To some people, I am kind of a Merlin who takes lots of crazy chances, but rarely makes mistakes. I've made some bad ones, but, fortunately, the successes have come along fast enough to cover up the mistakes. When you go to bat as many times as I do. you're bound to get a good average."

Finally, this author was an acquaintance of former Atlanta Brave's pitcher John Smoltz. In a discussion about him being a major league pitcher and defining his success, he shared a great perspective with me. He said that when he entered the league, his goal was not to win twenty games a year, or a Cy Young Award or many of the goals that you think about.

Rather, Smoltz said his goal was to give up 200 homeruns in his career. This may sound like a strange goal, but the logic behind it is sound. His goal was to have a long successful career. If he only played a couple of seasons, he could never give up 200 homeruns, but if he were to play for fifteen or twenty years then the possibility of giving up that many homeruns was almost a given.

Ironically, Smoltz ended his career giving up 288 homeruns and losing 155 games. Both of these stats sound like a career full of failure. However, Smoltz had one of the most successful careers in baseball history. Besides the losses and the homeruns he gave up, note these other stats on his career. Smoltz is the only pitcher in history with over 200 wins and over 150 saves. He is a CY Young Award winner, World Series Champion, and after twenty-one years as a major league pitcher, he was inducted in the Hall of Fame.

Takeaway

What if Smoltz had viewed giving up homeruns as a fatal failure, rather than simply part of the path to a successful career? What if you had given up trying to walk as a toddler and remained crawling your entire life? Sounds silly, you might think. What else appears silly to you in your present adult life?

PERSPECTIVE 5: WE HIRE FOR STRENGTHS BUT MANAGE FOR WEAKNESSES

The irony of most hiring is that we seek out candidates who will bring value to the position. We look for people with a strong resume and talents that stand out. However, once we have this perfect candidate in place, the focus becomes more about improving performance or fixing weaknesses than it is about improving the strengths on which they were hired.

Story

One leader shared his experience as a first-year teacher in a large school system in Georgia. He was looking forward to bringing his talents and strengths to his new job. However, within the first few weeks of school, he was given something called a PAC, which was a personal appraisal cycle that was meant for him to focus on areas of improvement for the school year. So, he was basically required to spend his first-year teaching focusing on two or three areas that he felt needed improvement.

This is not a unique situation when you consider that most employees are evaluated with a performance review, which usually focuses on areas of growth, which is just a nice way to say weaknesses.

However, author of *New York Times'* best-selling book *The Carrot Principle*, Chester Elton, suggests that we need to focus on more than just areas of improvement. He suggests that aspirational conversations are more productive. He said to get the best out of your employees you have to know them and what motivates them.

There are five key questions to ask staff on a regular basis, in place of the event, such as employee review (a review ultimately focused on what they need to work on, or a focused set of questions regarding employee improvement). In education, this suggests formative assessment (ongoing, interim) in place of summative assessment (the test, the autopsy to determine if one passed or failed). These five questions become more productive.

1) Have we kept our promises to you?
2) What do you think we do really well, such as at school do we do reading, extra-curricular activities, and so on?
3) What do you see in other schools that would make us do better?
4) What would make you want to leave us?
5) Where do you see yourself in three to five years? People often leave because there is no room to grow. Ask them what is their vision. Does one

desire to work toward an administrative role, and so on. Tell them you will help them get there. An education example, just be the best teacher you can be every day for me and I will help you achieve your goals.

Takeaway

What difference do you see in this approach? Can this shift from a focus on employee improvement to employee strengths and how you can further support them create an ultimate difference in results? Can this invigorate your workforce?

PERSPECTIVE 6: KNOWLEDGE IS NO LONGER POWER

In the past, especially before the technology explosion, knowledge was power. For centuries, we have all known that knowledge is power. The basic management hierarchy of almost all organizations is based on this premise. The top person in any company knows the vision, he or she shares that down, and so forth. Along these lines knowledge becomes very powerful.

Your boss knows about something, a big change that will take place next month, but she can't share it with you, just yet. You want that information. You want to know how it will affect your job, your life, the organization, your coworkers, and so on.

Your boss' boss knows a little more, and your boss wants to know what his or her boss knows. This is how most organizational leadership still runs on a daily basis. They squeeze every drop of power out of the knowledge they held.

Most information doesn't need to be on a need-to-know basis. And in many cases, when leaders hold "their cards close to the vest," then it's usually to make themselves feel more important or powerful.

However, effective leaders find it more beneficial to pass along knowledge quickly so their teams can use that knowledge to help the organization gain a competitive advantage. Speed of knowledge is the new measure of power!

In the information age, the world of knowledge is moving very fast. If you sit on knowledge for a moment, it could end up being useless because someone else will beat you to the punch.

Story

Jason Jennings, best-selling author and speaker, shared an example of this concept when he spent with the Koch Brothers gathering information for his research. At the end of their visit, Charles Koch told him that he could take a copy of their five-year strategic plan to look over for any information that he needed.

Jason asked, "Don't you want me to sign a non disclosure?" Charles replied, "No, in fact we send a copy of this out to our competitors to let them know how and when they are going to die." He was joking, of course, but his point was that it is not the knowledge that makes them successful, but that it is the execution of it.

Charles went on to tell him that he felt sorry for Jason because he was so old. And Jason replied, "What do you mean? I am not even as old as you." Charles said, "Only old people believe that knowledge is power. One time knowledge was power, when not everyone had access to it. But everyone has access to it now, so there is no need to try and keep from everyone. Especially within an organization."

Charles said, "It is not knowledge that is power now, but that flawless execution is power now. And the more people in your organization that have the knowledge or are 'In the know,' the more likely you are to have flawless execution, because everyone is on the same page."

Jason said he was interviewing the Smuckers brothers and asked them if he needed to sign a non-disclosure? Tim Smucker replied, "What type of people do you hang out with?" He said, "No, you don't need to sign anything, in fact, we have our strategic plan available to anyone who wants to see it. This reinforced the idea to Jason that it is not knowledge that is power anymore, but it is how the power is used, that is, flawless execution!"

Jason went on to share that he believes in today's culture that knowledge kept in secrecy, or the holding on to knowledge, is the currency of the unproductive. These are the people who only have value because of the secrets they know. They are unproductive, they do very little, but people are afraid of them because they know all the secrets.

He shared that leaders may keep secrets because it gives them a sense of self-importance, or they are afraid the competition will know what they are up to. But great leaders understand that it's not knowledge but execution of knowledge that makes organizations successful.

Takeaway

Knowledge is no longer power. Rather than trying to hoard something that can be easily acquired, share your knowledge. Two people will collectively know more than one. Three will know more than two. And when you have a room full of smart people sharing their knowledge, there's very little you can't accomplish together. The flawless execution of knowledge is powerful.

PERSPECTIVE 7: PLANNING AHEAD . . . IN REVERSE

Backward planning or as the authors call it "Planning Ahead . . . in Reverse" is a great tool to help achieve your goals. Time management and organization are two areas, which can add to the stress level of any leader. So, learning how to plan backward can help alleviate some of the stress that you might typically encounter when preparing for a new initiative. It is what Stephen Covey called "planning with the end in mind."

The idea is to start with your event, goal, or initiative in mind and then work backward from there to develop your plan. By starting at the end and looking back, you can mentally prepare yourself for success, map out the specific milestones you need to reach, and identify where in your plan you have to be particularly energetic or creative to achieve the desired results.

Backward planning, however, is more than reversing the direction of your traditional plan. It's about adopting a different perspective and, perhaps, identifying different milestones as a result. It's a great supplement to traditional planning, and it gives you a much fuller appreciation of what it may take to achieve success.

Most leaders have a mode of thinking that is based on *forecasts* (What do we think is going to happen?) rather than on *visions* (What do we want to happen?). So ideally, we would want to focus on our vision, what we want to happen and then plan backward to achieve the vision.

While it may not seem like there would be much difference between planning forward to a goal versus planning backward from a goal, it is similar to editing a piece of writing. If you edit it by simply reading it, then you may get caught up in the story itself and miss crucial errors. But if you read the piece backward, starting with the last sentence, then it's easier to focus on grammar and spelling errors without getting caught up in the story.

Another factor is the human element. When a new initiative or event is planned or product is developed, you have to know whom it affects. If you don't plan backward, you could run into a situation where unrealistic time lines or work requirements will occur. For instance, if you need employees to work a lot of overtime for an extended period of time, then you haven't properly planned.Preparing backward will force you to put more time and effort into your planning initially, but will hopefully alleviate many pitfalls that may otherwise arise.

Story

A great example of backward planning comes in the field of politics. Todd Rehm is a political consultant and pollster based in Atlanta, Georgia. Todd has helped dozens of candidates run effective political campaigns. He shared his insight into how he actually prepares a political campaign in reverse to make the most of time, money, and manpower.

Todd said there are many reasons that make planning in reverse the most appropriate method for political campaigns. It really lends itself to this type of planning because the election date is a set date with the end result. So everything culminates at that point. Planning from that point in reverse helps you create a road map to the destination.

First, when you plan in reverse, it helps you manage money. Todd said, "Most political campaigns don't have an endless supply of money, and if you don't plan with the Election Day in mind, many candidates will run out of money by the end of campaign when they need it to the most. The last few days of a campaign are usually the most important, because this is when its most [critical] and when you will make the biggest impact on the person going to the voting booth. So, you need to make sure your plan has a set amount of money for the last week or so, and then you start planning backwards on how to spend the money."

Todd explained that he uses spreadsheets to map out the campaign from the election date backward. Planning with the end in mind allows you to make adjustments as you move through an election. Most politicians like knocking on doors and talking to people, but if they don't have a great plan mapped out then there is no way to tell if you are being effective or not.

If you don't have targets or milestones targeted backward, then you may become overwhelmed or have no idea if you are on track. Now, you may hit all your milestones and still lose, but if you don't hit your milestones, then you are almost guaranteed to lose.

The only way to know what you have to do is figure out your tasks, and map out the time to complete each one from the end date. This also will help you know when best to start your campaign.

This is hard to do if you start planning as you go along. For example, if you need to reach 5,000 people in a district, then your plan may include knocking on 250 doors a week for twenty weeks. Well, you have to realize that campaign workers tend to be shy and may only meet 100 or 150 people the first week or two. So, if you are just planning as you go then this may seem overwhelming and even cause panic. But if you plan backward, you take this into account and have it set up for 150 people the first two weeks and then increase it to 260 or 270 people for the remaining weeks.

The human element becomes another reason to plan in reverse, for example, the energy level of the candidate. Todd shared, "You have to build in down time, so that they can keep their health up and [this downtime] allows them to build in time for breaks or even a vacation. If you don't have this planned out from the beginning, then they may not be able to keep up the pace and may get sick or at least have no energy at the end of the campaign when you need it the most."

Planning in reverse allows you to pace the candidates and even the campaign workers so everyone stays energized. And this can be true of any organization trying to complete a project or event, you have to make sure people don't burn out.

Takeaway

When planning an event, goal, or new initiative, begin with the end in mind. Picture what you want it to look like, then work backward to identify what needs to be done and when, in order to achieve your vision. Investing a little time to do this up front will significantly increase the likelihood that you get the desired result you envisioned from the beginning. It may save you money and time, and prevent overworking employees!

As a Marine, the author recognized that forward planning worked better with a near-term plan facing an ever-changing environment. The trap of forward planning may for some be that it "feels" natural as a go to. However, reverse planning better served long-term goals, emphasizing the vision previously featured here as a focus. Those planning on hiring a vet may often note a veteran's experience with planning to act, and then acting on the plan.

Chapter 4

Questions to Invite Expanding One's Leader Waistline

Taking thought from the previous reading, questions that can serve to expand one's leadership gut, one's perspective, such that one sees more possibilities for action in the moment, amid changing situations, possibilities that can be more productive for relationships and for results, include the following.

Motivation

How often do I hear myself say "can do" in my inner voice, inner speak?

How often do I hear my voice inside say "can't do?"

What do people think they hear—can do or can't do—who know me well?

Do I recognize and encourage the use of humor among others to lighten a situation, to keep people's thinking free and open?

How often do people laugh around me? How often do I laugh?

How might either my frowning/smiling (circle one's facial predisposition) influence my conversations with others?

Do I more often stand talking to others in daily interactions when the others are seated?

Do I verbally (and naturally) thank others as part of my normal conversations?

When is the last time I recall thanking another for something specific?

Am I comfortable/uncomfortable (circle your inclination here) verbally thanking and specifically noting what I am appreciating?

Does my office/work space appear more like all work and no play?

Does my office display color and conversation pieces—evidence of hobbies, where I have been on vacations, family/events/life milestones?

Visionary/Strategic Thinking

What purpose does story-telling and speaking using analogies serve?

What are the benefits of drawing as a visual aid during problem-solving conversation?

Do I frequently invite external person or people into my team meetings? What benefit does that give my team?

Which is my preference—to begin a question asking "Why. . .?" or "What. . .?" Or "How. . .?"

Regarding previous question, what do people who know me well say I more often lead off when asking?

Do I as naturally shift to asking the same question in a different way, or do I always ask questions the same way (like multiple choice)?

How can asking the same question in a different way prompt different ideas/ responses, from which to consider and create more alternative solutions?

Risk-Taking/Decisiveness

How often do I ask questions like "What's the worst that can happen?" in order to more quickly weigh pros and cons of a situation, seeking creative, thoughtful alternatives and possibilities?

Do I practice reverse role-play conversations to promote broader perspectives and accelerate people's confidence in deciding and taking risks?

Do I more often say something like "Here's the situation, let's talk" or "Here's the situation, and here's what I will do unless I hear from you by (4 pm local)?"

How much time, energy, certainty, ego do I invest—if it's not perfect, I don't want my name attached?

Do I factor self-fatigue and the fatigue of others around me, when making important or key decisions?

Resolving Conflicts

Do I focus on what is said and done during the conflict, without considering factors immediately preceding the conflict?

Do I tend to wear a chip on my shoulder and ensure people know when they messed up? Or do my behaviors, my outward manifestation of my inner attitude and thinking, characterize a return to courteous, cordial, and calm following a conflict?

What helps me to more quickly increase a space between the experience of an unpleasant impulse or event, and my reaction or response to the impulse or event? (The idea of creating a space in the moment, thinking on one's feet, to create more choices from which to respond beyond strictly flight or fight. One example of increasing a space, remember the use of "what" or "how" questions over "why" questions.)

Before saying "No," do I offer alternatives? (One example, saying, "Can you do this part? I'll do that part.")

Coaching Customer/Client Focus

"What is it you most want to have happen? How can I support you?" Would my clients indicate I communicate those messages to them?

In a crisis, do I maintain communication with my customer? (For example, "Here's what we've done so far, I continue seeking an answer.")

When my team is at fault, am I urgent and do I show urgency toward the customer?

Do I find ways to leave something positive with the customer—some new insight, an interesting article—leave something with them?

People do business with people they like. Do I seek the relationship first, the capabilities second? If people buy on relationship first, am I responsive? Do I promptly return their calls?

Coaching

Do others feel guilty for seeking me out, because I appear so constantly busy/preoccupied with the details?

Procrastination and focusing on little things are the opposites of acting on vision and risk-taking. The little things will always keep coming, keeping me otherwise preoccupied. Do I allow my focusing on little things to create a perception of inaccessibility?

Do I more frequently coach in terms of "what to do" or in terms of "what not to do?" Am I characterized by saying "Hold on to the ball" or "Don't fumble the ball?" What would others say I do more often?

How does communicating "what to do" affect motivation, strategic thinking, and productive conversations/overall momentum?

How does communicating "what to do" promote the risk-taking and decisiveness of others around me?

How does communicating "what to do" influence the way I question others in coaching conversations? (For example, "What will you do differently next time?")

Team Orientation

If I were a fly on the wall in my department/organizational/team meetings, could I quickly identify the manager/leader?

Do various team members alternate facilitating the meetings? Alternate developing the agenda?

Do my department//team meetings begin with an opportunity for informal sharing by each participant? Do I then conduct business with a focus on "what we have learned" during reviews and debriefs?

Do I often introduce/present tasks we are assigned as a team as "how can we benefit?"

Do I communicate that if one fails, we all fail, in little ways, over time?

Does my team always update a missing team member and practice other interdependencies?

Is asking for help (ideas/suggestions/support) from others a common practice among my team?

What message do I send to new prospects to our team? Is it "Join us, and you'll get this?" (selfish orientation) or is it "Join us and here's what you are going to be part of?"

Do I encourage personal development and delegating? What would others say?

Communicating

Do I focus and ask myself, "What are people going to hear?" or strictly focus on "What am I going to say?"

Does saying "Yes, but" sound familiar to me? (or do I more often say "Yes, and. . .")

Do I more finger point and communicate blame ("You screwed up"), or do I more often express patience ("I might have done it this way")?

Do I usually talk typically about problems/issues, keeping my relationships with others shallow and problem-centric?

How do I verbally react to unpleasant surprises/disappointments? With vulgarity and displeasure, or "How fascinating?"

Do people often tell me I show a serious frown or display other unfriendly expressions or body posture?

Do I often feel my own face contorted and tense? (If yes, give your head a quick shake and shake it off—literally).

Trust

When I meet people for the first time, is trust a given up front, or do people first to have to earn my trust?

If I believe trust must first be earned, and if my perception becomes my projection, could my belief cause me to think or act in a way that influences others to respond such that their actions reinforce the belief that trust must first be earned?

Can I be promoting a prove-it mentality by putting others on the defensive? Could they be feeling/thinking I'm going to catch them in a lie, in a mistake?

Leadership

What defines my leadership?
Do I effectively and genuinely connect with other human beings?
What are my top three leadership strengths?
How could I use them to further develop my overall leadership?
Am I more concerned about doing things right, or about doing the right thing?

Conclusion

My Eagle Has Landed—What's My View?

The eagle consumes live food. As an eagle, it pays to occasionally soar again, and to land in a different spot, with the benefit of a different view.

Taking this expanded perspective into everyday thinking and conversations, what might I discover? What might I appreciate? What might I take away for my ultimate winged flight?

Among takeaways that come to mind are questions . . . the kind of questions that are more powerful than the answers to guide me in immediate future decisions.

Questions to prompt our thinking interspersed around our stories serve as keepers as you choose. Refer to them and let them live with you, informing your leadership. What leadership questions do you the reader want to ask in a future or ongoing mentoring conversation with another as a result of reflecting on the stories here?

There is a power in the question that does not lie in the answer. What is more important right in this moment, doing things right, or doing the right thing?

One of the lessons realized and revisited as a result of writing this book comes in the form of this. As servant leadership gets described through the stories within, the servant leadership you choose to manifest serves independent of one's personal style. However, personal style informed more by intention to serve and encourage/model and less through control and admonish/lecture can only create a style unique to you. God Bless.

"I am not called to be successful. I am called to be faithful."—Mother Teresa

About the Authors

Marty Zimmerman is married with two daughters and a growing family of four grandchildren; he enjoys living in Michigan. A Naval Academy alum and Marine Corps veteran, he also served as a leadership/executive development coach in a Fortune 100 company and later operated his own business. He has enjoyed coaching leaders through the years in their 360 leadership performance feedback. Zimmerman additionally served as a secondary schools literacy consultant, coaching teachers and modeling literacy strategies for students at various schools. Earning two master's degrees in education (curriculum & instruction with a minor in reading, and in educational leadership), he currently enjoys teaching online and collaborating with faculty at Concordia University, Portland, and elsewhere. Zimmerman previously authored a leadership best practice book, *In Their Presence: Best Practices and Stories of Role Models*, in 2003. He appears as a fellow contributor with other professionals, including Jack Canfield, Stephen Covey, and Ken Blanchard, in *Speaking of Success* and *The Best of the Best*. He enjoys jogging and swimming to complement his habit of eating ice cream. Zimmerman hopes reading this book in partnership with Dr. Brad Johnson further beckons the participation and commitment of people to their leader's calling.

Dr. Brad Johnson is one of the most dynamic and engaging speakers in the fields of education and leadership. He is an established author with books including *Learning on Your Feet: Incorporating Physical Activity into the K-8 Classroom*, *The Edutainer: Connecting the Art & Science of Teaching*, and *From School Administrator to School Leader: 15 Keys to Maximizing Your Leadership Potential*. Besides his experiences in "The Trenches" as a teacher, curriculum director, and administrator, Dr. Johnson has served as an accreditation committee chair. He developed and supervised a formal mentoring program. He has also served on board-level educational committees. He recently spent several weeks in Malaysia training teachers for their Ministry of Education. Dr. Johnson currently serves on the national faculty of Concordia University's School of Graduate Studies where he teaches courses in leadership.